822·33

Items should be returned on or before the date shown below. Items
not already requested by other borrowers may be renewed in person,
in writing or by telephone. To renew, please quote the number on the
barcode label. To renew online a PIN is required. This can be requested
at your local library.
Renew online @ www.dublincitypubliclibraries.ie
Fines charged for overdue items will include postage incurred in recovery.
Damage to or loss of items will be charged to the borrower.

Comhairle Cathrach
Bhaile Átha Cliath
Dublin City Council

**Leaeharlanna Poiblí
Chathair Bhaile Átha
Cliath**

Due Date	Due Date	Due Date
Brainse Rátheanaigh Raheny Branch Tel: 8315521		

SHAKESPEARE
&
MATURE LOVE

how to get from nature to love in Shakespeare

Roger Peters

**Quaternary
Imprint**

Shakespeare & Mature Love
how to get from nature to love in Shakespeare

Shakespeare & Mature Love
is a companion volume to Volumes 1, 2, 3 and 4
of *William Shakespeare's Sonnet Philosophy* (2005)
and *Shakespeare's Global Philosophy* (2017)

ISBN 978-0-473-39502-5 (pbk)
ISBN 978-0-473-39503-2 (hbk)
ISBN 978-0-473-39504-9 (epub)

Page setup by Maree Horner

QUATERNARY IMPRINT
Published for the Quaternary Institute
www.quaternaryinstitute.com

Maree

Contents

Preface

While writing a summary volume in 2009 for the 1760-page, four volume *William Shakespeare's Sonnet Philosophy* (2005), a closer look at sonnet 32 alerted me to the extraordinary level of intentionality in Shakespeare's understanding and expression of love. What is this mature form of love that locates itself beyond the conventional forms of love such as the Romantic, Idealistic, Christian, etc.

To consider the implications of the deeper insights into mature Shakespearean love, I put aside the summary volume to write the essay that forms the basis of this book. With sonnet 32's claim repeated in sonnet 80, and with natural or Shakespearean love suffusing the set of 154 sonnets – beyond style, form, favour or rhyme – there arose the opportunity to complement the philosophical arguments and evidence from the *Sonnets* with their unprecedented depth of emotional expression and insight, all from the same nature-based understanding.

After all, Shakespeare writes his philosophy deliberately in a set of love sonnets to show the connectivity between consistent human rationality and the depths of emotional resources humans experience. Shakespeare seems to make palpable the living relationship between heart and mind. He does so at a depth that enables many to intuit a profoundly liberating quality in the set of sonnets.

While most of the significant insights have been incorporated back into the summary volume, the idea of mature Shakespearean love is such a significant one it warrants a stand-alone publication to emphasise its timelessness and relevance to the contemporary global constituency.

Roger Peters 2017

32

IF thou furuiue my well contented daie,
When that churle death my bones with duſt ſhall couer
And ſhalt by fortune once more re-ſuruay:
Theſe poore rude lines of thy deceaſed Louer:
Compare them with the bett'ring of the time,
And though they be out-ſtript by euery pen,
Reſerue them for my loue, not for their rime,
Exceeded by the hight of happier men.
Oh then voutſafe me but this louing thought,
Had my friends Muſe growne with this growing age,
A dearer birth then this his loue had brought
To march in ranckes of better equipage:
    But ſince he died and Poets better proue,
    Theirs for their ſtile ile read,his for his loue.

1 Philosophy and love

If William Shakespeare's sonnets contain a substantial philosophy, what does he mean when he says they will be read for their love rather than for their style? What depth of love does Shakespeare experience if he can make such a self-conscious claim?

Why, we might ask, are Shakespeare's sonnets regarded near universally as the greatest love sonnets in English literature or any literature? And what makes Romeo and Juliet the most famous play about star-crossed lovers? What accounts for the deeply moving expression of love Shakespeare infuses into his works?

For more than a decade I had been delving into the philosophy structured by Shakespeare into his *Sonnets* of 1609[1]. Early in the process I realised I was looking at what could only be an intentional arrangement of the 154 sonnets into a meaningful set with two clearly defined internal sequences and a number of further levels of deliberate demarcation[2].

As the evidence accumulated it was difficult to avoid the implication that Shakespeare publishes his collected sonnets around twenty years after he starts writing plays to present the nature-based philosophy behind all his plays and longer poems.

The discovery of a substantial philosophy in the sonnet set has determined my researches over the last number of years. Only recently did I turn my attention to the possibility that the love talked about so frequently in the sonnets[3] and recognized by so many of Shakespeare's readers for its unmatched veracity, vivacity and maturity is also intentionally configured into the set.

It is as if Shakespeare anticipates those who would find the quality of love he embodies in the sonnets wonderfully congruent with their deepest emotional experiences. In other words Shakespeare says blatantly he expects his set of sonnets to be regarded above all others for their expression of love and gives the reasons why.

---

[1] *The 1760 pages of the four volume set 'William Shakespeare's Sonnet Philosophy' (hereafter 'WSSP') examines in some detail the logical structure of the 154 sonnets and its implications for Shakespeare's plays. Some material is also available on the website: www.quaternaryinstitute.com* (Roger Peters, *William Shakespeare's Sonnet Philosophy*, Quaternary Imprint, Kaponga, 2005.)

[2] *We can note that there is an increasing acceptance by scholars and others that Shakespeare was responsible for the arrangement of the 1609 edition. From the evidence of the plays, Shakespeare was writing sonnets in the early 1590s, so there is reason to think he devoted time, possibly in the years before 1609, to organising his existing sonnets into the 154-sonnet set. Two sonnets, 138 and 144, which were originally published in 1599 in a collection of poems 'The Passionate Pilgrim' by William Jaggard, are altered significantly so it is not difficult to imagine Shakespeare reworking and adding sonnets as the set achieved its definitive state. Shakespeare was not unique in refining his sonnets. Michael Drayton first published his sonnet set 'Idea in Sixty Three Sonnets' in 1594 and was still revising it in 1621.*

[3] *The word 'love' in its various forms is mentioned around 200 times in the sonnets and over 3000 times in Shakespeare's complete works.*

This essay will follow the structure of the philosophy in the set of 154 sonnets step by step. By adhering to the patently visible patterns in the 1609 edition we should be able to watch Shakespeare as he develops his understanding of deep and abiding human love in nature. The evidence of the 154 sonnets should establish the enduring grounds on which he bases his emotive comedies, histories and tragedies that move so many to read and perform them thousands of times worldwide on any one day.

2 Loving and hating Shakespeare

Why is it so easy to misrepresent Shakespearean love?

The response to Shakespeare's love sonnets over the last 400 years has rarely been without quibbles and moans. Commentators voice both admiration and concern while editors reorder them, anthologize only those they like and alter the meanings of dozens of apparently puzzling words. And the plays are given the same querulous treatment.

Why, for instance, is William Wordsworth attracted one minute and repulsed the next when he reads about love in the sonnets[4]? Why do I get the feeling the film *Shakespeare in Love* cheats and cheapens by suggesting Shakespeare got it all from a London mistress – like clap?

Surely there is more to it than that. Is the love Shakespeare sublimates into his poems and plays Platonic, homosexual, Christian, Romantic, erotic, stoic or cynical? Readers with one or other of these sensibilities are attracted to Shakespeare's oeuvre even if, like Wordsworth, they find some works, or parts of works, anathema.

The attraction can be quite equivocal as when those with Christian sympathies are drawn to parts that seem more Christian but have to admit there is no evidence generally to suggest Shakespeare was a Christian. Yet to explain their fascination with the works they insinuate he could have been a Christian in private[5]. The deep

---

[4] *Wordsworth complains that 'these sonnets beginning at 127 to his mistress are worse than a puzzle-peg. They are abominably harsh, obscure, and worthless. The others are for the most part much better, have many fine lines and passages. They are also in many places warm with passion. Their chief faults, and heavy ones they are, are sameness, tediousness, quaintness, and elaborate obscurity'.* (Wordsworth's marginal note in: Robert Anderson, *The Works of the British Poets*, Edinburgh and London, 1792-95.)

[5] *In his 'Shakespearean Tragedy' Raymond Bradley acknowledges Shakespeare's tragedies are 'secular' rather than Christian yet he still prefaces his comments with the proviso Shakespeare may 'as a private person, had a religious faith' and that 'his tragic view can hardly have been in contradiction with this faith' (p 30).* (Raymond Bradley, *Shakespearean Tragedy*, London, St Martin's Press, 1904.)

Blair Leishman in 'Themes and Variations' acknowledges the lack of references to matters Christian or Platonic in the sonnets, yet still suggests that if Shakespeare was asked about the omission he would have replied 'Well, fancy that now! To tell you the truth, I just hadn't noticed' (p 177). (J. B. Leishman, *Themes and Variations in Shakespeare's Sonnets*, London, Hutchinson, 1961.)

And Stephen Booth in 'Shakespeare's Sonnets', says it is 'unreasonable and unprofitable to argue that sonnet 146 does not espouse an orthodox Christian position' (p 514). Booth says he does not want to 'homogenise' the experience of the poem by combining the seemingly opposed views. Instead, he suggests disingenuously that Shakespeare's poetry is designed to accommodate irreconcilable readings. (Stephen Booth, *Shakespeare's Sonnets*, Yale University Press, 2000.)

As a rule of thumb, editors and commentators reveal their ignorance of the inherent philosophy in Shakespeare's plays and poems when they attribute the whole or parts of his works to other authors or any form of religion. Instead, by identifying a specific author or religion, the editors and commentators reveal their own level of intellectuality relative to

irony is that the intentional Christian references are no more than instances where Shakespeare holds fundamental Christian prejudices up for scrutiny[6].

We have to ask, then, assuming Shakespeare is the nature poet who holds a mirror to nature more than any other poet[7], how is he able to give such a natural voice to the heady heights of religious-like love. What is Shakespeare doing to galvanize our deepest emotions when he seems to work with such a resolutely earthy palette? Or, to put it another way, how much of the brilliant philosophy Shakespeare incorporates into his love sonnets needs to be understood before we can fully experience the mature love he embeds in his verse?

---

the genius they acknowledge is Shakespeare's. An editor, for instance, who attributes parts of a play such as 'Measure for Measure' to Thomas Middleton, exhibits intelligence similar to the inferior playwright.

[6] *I present the evidence for Shakespeare's critique of male-based religious prejudices in 'WSSP' and in 'Shakespeare's Gobal Philosophy',* Quaternary Imprint, 2017.

[7] *Samuel Johnson recognises that 'Shakespeare is, above all other writers, at least above all modern writers, the poet of* **nature***; the poet that holds up to his readers a faithful mirror of manners and of life' (p 508).* (Preface to Shakespeare, Samuel Johnson, *Lives of the Poets,* London, Frederick Warne, ND.)

3 Calling on nature

What sort of mirror, then, does Shakespeare hold to nature to reflect our deepest feelings of love? How is he able to construct a set of profoundly intelligent sonnets using words and numbers to provide a beguiling expression of love based in nature?

On the surface, the 154 sonnets can seem a miscellany of competing styles. What is the relationship between the very literal 'increase' sonnets that begin the set and sonnet 18 with its apparent combination of the romantic and ideal? Then there are sonnets like 31 that proscribe 'dear (read 'costly') religious love', sonnet 116 that speaks of a 'marriage of true minds', sonnet 129 that excoriates 'murdrous' lust, sonnets 135 and 136 that between them wordplay the name 'Will' nineteen times, sonnet 146 that ascribes to the soul a dead dead death, and the final two sonnets, 153 and 154, that augment an erotic Roman epigram.

We have to go back to the beginning and work our way in from the overall structure of the 1609 *Sonnets* to see just what Shakespeare means when he says his sonnets will be remembered for their 'love', as he does specifically in sonnets 32 and 80[8]. We will also refer to the plays where appropriate to reinforce the development of our exposé of Shakespearean love[9].

Not only do many readers recognize Shakespeare anecdotally as a nature poet, his contemporaries, in the poems and prefaces they wrote in his honour, celebrate his acceptance of nature as primary[10]. So, the decisive move is to acknowledge that

---

[8] *Sonnet 32 provides a vivid avowal of Shakespeare's expectation for his own poetry:*
> And though they be out-stripped by every pen,
> Reserve them for my **love**, not for their **rhyme**, (*sonnet 32, 6-7*)

And in the couplet the Poet asks the youth to talk of him in these terms:
> But since he died and Poets better prove,
> Theirs for their **style** I'll read, his for his **love**. (*sonnet 32, 13-14*)

In sonnet 80, Shakespeare reiterates the difference between his poetry and that of others:
> O how I faint when I of you do write,
> Knowing **a better spirit doth use your name**,
> And in the praise thereof spends all his might,
> To **make me tongue-tied speaking of your fame**. (*sonnet 80, 1-4*)
> ....
> Then if he thrive and I be cast away,
> **The worst was this, my love was my decay**. (*sonnet 80, 13-14*)

[9] *All play references are to the 1623 'Folio' as all other editions since make unwarranted changes to the text. The line numbering is continuous from play beginning to play end. Similarly, as the 1609 edition of Shakespeare's 'Sonnets' is the original text, all the modern English renditions of the sonnets provided in this essay are offered on the proviso the 1609 edition is the default text. A facsimile of the 1609 edition is essential for appreciating how Shakespeare structures his philosophy into the set and achieves his mature expression of love.*

[10] 'Who, as he was a happy imitator of **nature**, was a most gentle expresser of it'. (John Heminge, Henry Condell, *Mr. William Shakespeare's Comedies, Histories and Tragedies*, 1623.)
'Next, **nature** only helped him'. (Leonard Digges, *Shakespeare's Poems*, 1640.)

Shakespeare grounds his philosophy in nature. As we will see, for Shakespeare there is nothing more basic than nature as the philosophic ground or given, not God or any other super-natural entity born in the human imagination[11].

As we consider the 154 sonnets in their 1609 edition, we will see that the unique arrangement of the set lends support to the testimony of Shakespeare's contemporaries. The collection of 154 sonnets makes most sense if the complete set is seen as representing nature. Only nature, which appears sixteen times throughout (thirteen of which refer to nature at large), has the pedigree to be the unquestioned given out of which all else develops.

Our expectation that the 154-sonnet set represents nature is reinforced when it is realised the number 154 adds numerologically to unity: $154 = 1+5+4 = 10 = 1+0 = 1$[12]. This suggests Shakespeare compiled 154 sonnets intentionally so his set could represent the singularity of nature.

The unique singularity of 'nature' in the *Sonnets* accords with the everyday usage of the word nature. Nature, unlike the words God, universe or world, is not referred to in the plural – except metaphorically when characterising the multiplicity of human 'natures'. We do not readily talk of many or other natures as we do of many and other Gods, universes or worlds.

The singularity of nature does not have to be defined or enforced or capitalised as happens with the biblical God. The scribes who invented the monotheistic God allot the first three (more or less depending on the text or religion) Mosaic Laws to underwrite 'His' existence and underline his superiority and his draconian powers based in jealousy and vengeance[13].

Sardonically, maybe, Shakespeare numbers his sonnets with the relatively complex 154 to represent the singularity of undefinable nature to parody Dante Alighieri. Dante numbers the cantos of his *Divine Comedy* with the simpler 100 ($100 = 1+0+0 = 1$) or 'divine unity' to foster the illusion that, in his Mediterranean/subterranean sitcom, the tripartite God is indeed a one-man band[14]. Females such

[11] *Because all references to Gods and Goddesses are nominal, in that the words God/ Goddess vocalise sensations that are experienced undifferentiated in the depths of the human imagination – just as the word 'ouch' vocalizes externally induced sensations of pain – this essay follows the example of Shakespeare's Sonnets in giving all instances of the words God/Goddess a capital G.*

[12] *In sonnet 14, Shakespeare draws a logical line between his structural system that uses numbers to provide a common sense arrangement of the 154 sonnets, and all forms of astrology, alchemy or other arcane practices that use numbers to speculate about the heavens, stars or future. Anyone inclined to view Shakespeare's number system in an arcane sense will be completely at odds with the nature-based understanding of mature love he presents throughout his sonnet set and plays.*

[13] *A quick search of Wikipedia – as an encyclopedia edited continually by many hands – reveals no entries for 'natures' but references to Gods, universes and worlds. Similarly, and equally anecdotally, in dictionaries nature is ubiquitous whereas the Christian God is defined separately from other Gods.*

[14] *The numbering system in the 'Divine Comedy' is discussed in*: William Anderson, *Dante the Maker*, London, Routledge and Kegan Paul, 1980.

as Mary, Eve, and Dante's sweetheart Beatrice, are kept at arm's length from daddy's lazy-boy.

On Shakespeare's dramatic stage, recourse to ubiquitous nature is the basis from which he displays or resolves the interplay of love and hate. Throughout Shakespeare's histories and tragedies, the biblical male-God or any overly idealised male, when believed in literally is identified as the root cause of love-hate divisiveness. In telling contrast, in his comedies, eleven canny females and three savvy males stage-manage the action to achieve a nature-based resolution of love and hate[15].

The organisation of the thirty-six plays in the 1623 *Folio* provides the clue. The fourteen comedies are led either by females (eleven) who correct male-based disorders, or by males (three) who have matured their feminine and masculine personae[16]. In stark contrast all the ten histories and twelve tragedies are fronted by God-driven males or the like who lead their casts into mayhem or death and murder. Because they are generic, none of the *Folio* comedies have characters named in the titles, yet all the histories and tragedies name the culpable or fated male.

As we follow Shakespeare into the 154 sonnets we will see he recognises the originary status of the human female over the male in nature as the foundation for an enduring rehabilitation of love over hate.

Shakespeare uniquely includes 154 sonnets in his set so the whole set can represent nature. Accepting nature as the unconditional given provides the foundation for understanding and experiencing Shakespearean love.

---

[15] *In the eleven comedies in which females correct unnatural male-based beliefs or customs, we watch as Helena runs rings round Bertram in 'All's Well that Ends Well', the Princess of France reduces the King of Navarre to crocodile tears in 'Love's Labour's Lost', Mrs. Page/ Mrs. Ford get the dirty laundry on Falstaff in 'The Merry Wives of Windsor', Viola plays God to reverse-psychologise Orsino in 'Twelfth Night', Rosalind mind-wrestles Orlando in 'As You Like It', Hermione/Paulina display the powdered phallus for Leontes in 'The Winter's Tale', Portia foists a bloodless coup on Shylock in 'The Merchant of Venice', Julia/Silvia have the speed on Proteus in 'The Two Gentlemen of Verona', Beatrice shows Benedick the ape in 'Much Ado About Nothing', Hermia trumps her sado-masochistic father in 'A Midsummer Night's Dream' and Amelia the Abbess goes monastery to give Egeon a taste of purgatory in 'The Comedy of Errors'.*

In the three comedies where mature males direct the action, Petruchio restores Katherine's feminine/masculine balance in 'The Taming of the Shrew', Vincentio returns Vienna to sexual and mental sanity in 'Measure for Measure' and Prospero corrects the male-based prejudices of his Italian colleagues in 'The Tempest'.

[16] *As this essay develops we will follow the trail of feminine and masculine personae in the sonnets to show at the end how the sexual differentiation of female and male has its counterpart in the feminine and masculine gender dispositions of the mind and why understanding the natural dynamic of the interrelationship is at the heart of Shakespearean love.*

4 Bringing on the female and male

When Shakespeare divides his set of 154 sonnets into two distinct sequences, one to the female and the other to the male, is he identifying the sexual dynamic in nature as the prerequisite for the intensified emotions we feel toward our parents, children and lovers?

Whatever the propriety of our first move in identifying the whole set with nature on the basis of internal and anecdotal evidence and the numerical architecture of the number 154, Shakespeare's next move certainly locates the two protagonists basic for the various forms of love between human beings. The two commonly recognized sequences within the set of 154 sonnets – based on the evident break between sonnets 126 and 127 – are the 126 sonnets to a male and the 28 sonnets to a female.

Significantly, Shakespeare seems to allocate the relationship of male and female in nature a logical function in his set of sonnets. Compared to the extensive and continual argument evident within the sonnets themselves, Shakespeare does not put forward an argument for the status of nature or the sexual dynamic of female and male. Rather, by having them provide the unquestioned overall structure of the set and the two sequences, they are the givens he installs before the possibility of love as we know it can develop.

In keeping with their function as givens, we hear nature referred to generically as the 'sovereign mistress' in sonnet 126, the female is called 'Mistress' six times in her sequence and the male called 'Master Mistress' in sonnet 20[17]. These generic names identify more nearly the logical function of the female and male in the sonnets than do the gossipy familiar 'dark lady' – the name does not occur in the sonnets – or the homo-genderised 'friend' – even though both female and male are called 'friend'. The chatty nick-names are pathological pseudonyms body-tagging grim attempts to turn the sonnet set into a psychodrama about Shakespeare's life.

The generic relationship of nature, female and male is further enhanced when we reckon the numbering of the internal sequences. We find the male has a

---

[17] *The placement of the generic names at nodal points in the 154 sonnets, and the absence of proper names, reinforces Shakespeare's determination to present an exacting and compelling philosophy of love.*

Sonnet 20 begins by identifying the male as having a 'woman's face' because in 'nature' he derives from the female. Hence the Poet calls the male 'Master Mistress' as he begins to elucidate the type of 'passion' or love he feels for him:

A woman's face with nature's own hand painted,
Hast thou the **Master Mistress** of my passion, (*sonnet 20*, 1-2)

In the final sonnet of the male sequence, 126, the Poet identifies 'nature' as 'sovereign mistress'. It is she who brings the Master Mistress to 'audit':

If **Nature (sovereign mistress** over wrack) (*sonnet 126*, 5)

The first sonnet of the female sequence, sonnet 127, names the 'Mistress' as it is she who teaches the Poet throughout her sonnets:

Therefore my **Mistress'** eyes are Raven black, (*sonnet 127*, 9)

Sonnet 154 confirms the originary status of the female by naming her as the set draws to a close:

For men diseased, but I my **Mistress'** thrall, (*sonnet 154*, 12)

number 9: (126 = 1+2+6 = 9) and the female is numbered 1: (28 = 2+8 = 10 = 1+0 = 1). The implication is that the female is a unity but the male is not – he requires a further 1 to complete his unity: 9+1 = 10 = 1+0 = 1. So, the female is at one with nature whereas the male seems partially estranged (see sonnet 38).

Shakespeare signals his acceptance of generic female unity and male disunity sixteen years before 1609 with the publication of an early exploration in his nature-based philosophy. In *Venus and Adonis* of 1593, Shakespeare corrects Ovid's male-controlled version of the long poem by putting the originary female in charge of the action. Venus challenges the recalcitrant male Adonis to mature his adolescent attitude to nature and so to her. Because Adonis refuses to accept Venus' arguments about his natural propensities, he is gored by a boar and dies irredeemably rooted in self-regard[18].

This is not the place to expand on the corroboration available in the *Folio* or *Venus and Adonis* for the role of nature and the female in the *Sonnets*. But, on the evidence cited so far, it seems Shakespeare presents his examination and expression of interpersonal love by first contextualising his account with the natural givens over which human beings have no control. He accepts the existence of nature and the sexual division into female and male as grounds or preconditions for the mature development of human love.

Shakespeare uniquely organises his 154-sonnet set to accommodate a sequence of 126 sonnets representing the male and 28 sonnets representing the female. Appreciating the originary status of the female in relation to the male and acknowledging both as natural givens is the next step toward appreciating Shakespearean love.

---

[18] *This essay is part of a larger case that Shakespeare held to the same nature-based philosophy throughout his life. Pertinent to the next section of the essay is the argument Shakespeare puts in Venus' mouth for the logic of increase:*

'Is thine own heart to thine own face affected?
Can thy right hand seize love upon thy left?
Then woo thyself, be of thy self rejected:
Steal thine own freedom, and complain on theft.
   Narcissus so him self him self forsook,
   And died to kiss his shadow in the brook.

'Torches are made to light, jewels to wear,
Dainties to taste, fresh beauty for the use,
Herbs for their smell, and sappy plants to bear.
Things growing to them selves, are growth's abuse,
   Seeds spring from seeds, and beauty breedeth beauty;
   Thou wast begot, to get it is thy duty.

'Upon the earth's increase why shouldst thou feed,
Unless the earth with thy increase be fed?
By law of nature thou art bound to breed,
That thine may live, when thou thyself art dead:
   And so in spite of death thou dost survive,
   In that thy likeness still is left alive'. (*Venus and Adonis*, 157-74)

5 No love without increase

What is the relevance to deep and abiding love of a definitive argument in the first fourteen sonnets about choosing to increase or not?

If Shakespeare recognises nature as the seamless backdrop for the love potential of the female and male (in order of achieved unity) how does he characterise the differences between female and male in their distinctive sequences? To better account for the differences we will examine more closely the sonnets dedicated to them.

If, starting at the first sonnet, we look for the word 'love' we find no mention until sonnet 3 where it appears conditionally as 'self love'. The male youth is accused of indulging in 'self love' if he spurns the logic of his natural inheritance from the female. Furthermore, all the first fourteen sonnets are dedicated to arguing that the adolescent male should recognize the biology of increase or the fact he was born of increase from a 'mother' (sonnet 3) and 'father' (sonnet 13)[19] with the potential to have children himself.

When we look again, we find the word 'increase' occurs in the first line of the first sonnet[20] and so precedes 'love' into the set. It does seem that Shakespeare, before he begins to tackle the issue of love, introduces increase as the natural consequence of the division of female and male in nature.

In confirmation, we find that the word 'love', as the emotional connection to another, does not enter the set until sonnet 9. As we read sonnet 9, we find it quite forthright in saying because self love is 'murd'rous'[21] there can be no love unless the youth recognizes the logic of increase. Shakespeare's determination to draw a logical line at this point is emphasised by the fact he does not introduce his sonnet writer as 'I', 'my' and 'me' until sonnet 10 and that sonnet 10 begins at the top of its page[22].

---

[19] *Sonnet 3 and 13 have the only mention of 'mother' or 'father' in the increase sonnets:*
   Thou art thy **mother**'s glass and she in thee
   Calls back the lovely April of her prime, (*sonnet 3*, 9-10)
   Sonnet 13 mentions son rather than daughter because the female is the source of increase:
   O none but unthrifts, dear my love you know,
   You had a **Father**, let your Son say so. (*sonnet 13*, 13-14)

[20] *The first sonnet, which introduces increase in its first line, anchors the set of individual sonnets back to the whole set with nature as given with its two internal sequences to the female and male:*
   From fairest creatures we desire **increase**,
   That thereby beauty's Rose might never die, (*sonnet 1*, 1-2)
   We will see that sonnet 14 is the last of the increase sonnets when it signals the transition from physical increase (called 'store') to the dynamic of the mind as 'truth and beauty'.

[21] *Sonnet 9, after encouraging the youth not to consume himself in 'single life', states the dire consequences for 'love' if he remains 'unused':*
   No love towards others in that bosom sits
   That on himself such **murd'rous shame commits**. (*sonnet 9*, 13-14)

[22] *If we look ahead we see that every twelfth sonnet from sonnet 10 onwards begins at the top of its page in the 1609 edition, Q. At the top and bottom of every other page in Q, the effected sonnets straddle from one page to the next by a variable number of lines. The*

Withholding the introduction of the first person of the writer until sonnet 10 is a situation completely unique in the sonnet sequences of Shakespeare's day. In every other sonnet sequence the love-sick romantic or idealistic 'I' or 'me' immediately avows self-serving love in the first sonnet[23].

It is the writer of the sonnets, identified as 'Poet' in sonnet 17, who is in a three-way love relationship with the Master Mistress and the Mistress. None of the three is allocated a personal or classical name, as in other love sequences of the time, suggesting they are generic characters representing female, male and Poet as archetypes. As we will see, the male youth and the mature female can also be read simultaneously as personae of the mature Poet's mind, or of anyone's mind.

Already, then, we are encountering something quite different in Shakespeare's love sonnets. Not only are both female and male addressed in the same set[24], interpersonal love is not mentioned until sonnet 9 and only after that does the Poet refer to himself in the first person.

As a set of love sonnets, Shakespeare's 1609 publication is revealing a double purpose. If we count the instances of 'love' throughout the 154 sonnets, fully 70 do not mention the word 'love', and 61 out of the 154 have no form of the word love. Indeed, some of the better known sonnets such as 12, 18, 24, 27, 44, 60, 74, 94, 127, 128, 129, 135 and 146 do not use 'love' or its derivatives, except for sonnet 18 that has one adverbial 'lovely'.

This suggests Shakespeare's sonnets, besides being 'love sonnets', give up half their number to reinforce the process of establishing a context for flourishing love. With a number of adjacent sonnets joined together as one by logical connectives such as 'but', 'thus' and 'so' – plus the sustained argument in the fourteen increase sonnets, and (as we will see) in sonnets 15 to 19 and the 'Alien' Poet group from sonnet 78 to 86 – this is no ordinary set of love sonnets.

The intentional inclusion or absence of the word 'love' across the 154 sonnets suggests the Poet of the set not only addresses the three-way love relationship between himself and the female and male, but as the philosophic author of the sonnets he lays down the logical preconditions for the possibility of love between female and male in nature and hence for any other form of love.

In keeping with Shakespeare's intentional mix of logic and love, after the three 'love's, one 'beloved' and one 'lovest' in sonnet 10, the love word appears only in sonnet 13 of the remaining increase sonnets. In sonnet 13, which complements sonnet 3 by adding 'father' to its 'mother', the love mentioned is again the murderous 'self love' that arises when the logic of increase is forgone.

---

resulting pattern of twelve twelve's from sonnet 10 to sonnet 153 suggests Shakespeare added a structure for time to his set. See 'WSSP'.

[23] *Every sonnet sequence included by Maurice Evans in 'Elizabethan Sonnets' begins with the first person in the first sonnet – even that by the only female poet he anthologises, Lady Mary Roth. (Maurice Evans, Elizabethan Sonnets, London, J. M. Dent, 1994.)*

[24] *This is another unique difference from his contemporaries who address exclusively either a female or a male.*

When we examine sonnet 11, we find it identifies the implications of refusing to accept the logic of increase. It states resolutely, if 'all were minded' like the selfish youth then in 'three score years' there would be no more human beings[25]. The use of such a logical argument should further prepare us for the rigour with which Shakespeare constructs his verse and dramas – yet still moves us deeply with his representation and expression of love.

Having structured his set with the unarguable givens – nature, female and male – Shakespeare's first fourteen sonnets introduce the issue over which the most crucial determination has to be made by humans en masse – to increase or not[26]. With the arrival of the ability to make conscious choices from out of the givens, a logical decision between 'self love' and 'love' determines the possibility for human survival.

Then, in the final increase sonnet 14[27], the youth is told that if he does not accept the logic of increase ('store') his – and everybody's – death would be the end of 'truth and beauty'[28]. Again the claim resounds with determined sense because, if all humans died without increasing, truth and beauty would reach its use-by-date and its products such as poetry would be but mute reminders of excessive idealistic conceits.

So, for Shakespeare, any system of thought that does not acknowledge the significance of increase before all else, excepting nature and the sexual dynamic,

---

[25] *Sonnet 11 addresses the logical consequence of 'all' males being like the youth and refusing to acknowledge the significance of increase. Shakespeare's critique is especially aimed at the celibacy of the clergy when it is promoted as the highest religious/civil ideal:*
> **If all were minded so,** the times should cease,
> And **threescore year would make the world away:** (*sonnet 11*, 7-8)

[26] *In Shakespeare's day, the epicene Christ was the exemplary model for the gold-standard of papal celibacy and, in our day, God-like nuclear Armageddon and irradiation are two of the most dramatic mind-games that threaten the logic of increase. The first indulges in macrocosmic one-upmanship and the other in microcosmic brinkmanship. In contrast, Shakespeare dramatises and poeticises 'common sense' (as Berowne insists in 'Love's Labour's Lost') as he plays directly with human nature in nature.*

[27] *As we will see, sonnet 14 is the last of the increase sonnets because sonnets 15 to 19 introduce a new topic – writing. Another measure of sonnet 14's role is its pivotal numbering. The number 14 divides evenly into 154 = 11, 28 = 2 and 126 = 9. The significance of the number 9 for the male sequence is apparent and the other numbers also have a significant function in the set. See 'WSSP'.*

[28] *Sonnet 14 interrelates the two-way logic that if there are no human beings then 'truth and beauty' is meaningless and that 'truth and beauty' gains its potential for meaningfulness from the sexual dynamic:*
> But from thine eies my knowledge I derive,
> And constant stars in them I read such art
> As **truth and beauty** shall together thrive
> **If from thy self, to store thou wouldst convert:**
>> Or else of thee this I prognosticate,
>> **Thy end is Truth's and Beauty's doom and date.** (*sonnet 14*, 9-14)

murders 'love' and kills 'truth and beauty'. Again, these seem incredibly forbidding constraints to put on the possibility of love.

As we follow Shakespeare in his explanation of the preconditions throughout the 154-sonnet set we might get a better idea of just what Shakespearean love entails and why it is so mature and free. We may then be able to account for the sharp-witted passion of Viola, Rosalind, Vincentio, Petruchio and the Princess of France – as just five of Shakespeare's canny and cunning lovers – and so get a dramatic measure of the depth and resilience of Shakespearean love[29].

We might then appreciate why Prospero tells Miranda, in the opening scenes of *The Tempest*, that his male-based rejection of her at birth dishonours increase because, under the custom of male-primogeniture, he believed there could be 'no worse' outcome[30]. His subsequent period of 'study' and recovery of natural female/feminine priority made him determine to ensure the love-match of Miranda and Ferdinand was a marriage of true minds[31].

So, just what type of love is it that Shakespeare seems to pinion resolutely to the sexual dynamic in nature and not to an idealized heaven or other extra human potentiality? As our account of the 154 sonnets unfolds we will have to answer this concern from those who hear some of the sonnets talk to their more romantic or idealistic dispositions.

Shakespeare begins his set of sonnets with fourteen sonnets that argue specifically for the logic of increase. Accepting increase as the precondition for love by reasoning beings opens the way for the development of mature Shakespearean love.

---

[29] From 'Twelfth Night', 'As You Like It', 'Measure for Measure', 'The Taming of the Shrew' and 'Love's Labour's Lost', respectively.

[30] *The full colon following* **'Princess:'** *in the 1623 Folio is crucial for the correct meaning of the passage. Most modern editions replace it with a comma:*
    Prospero: Thy mother was a piece of virtue, and
    She said thou wast my daughter; and thy father
    Was Duke of Milan, and **his only heir,**
    And Princess: no worse issued. (*Tempest*, 1.1.148-51)

[31] *Cordelia and Desdemona ('King Lear' and 'Othello') also acknowledge the logic of increase when their fathers challenge their willingness to love unconditionally. Both women avow half of their love to the father and half to the prospective husband as increase ensures that love survives across generations. The speech in which Cordelia avows her natural logic is panned by commentators as a formulaic response:*
    Cordelia: Good my Lord,
    You have **begot me, bred me,** loved me.
    I return those duties back as are right fit,
    Obey you, Love you, and most Honour you.
    Why have my Sisters' Husbands, if they say
    They love you all? Happily when I shall wed,
    That Lord, whose hand must take my plight, shall carry
    Half my love with him, half my Care, and Duty,
    Sure I shall never marry like my Sisters. (*King Lear*, 1.1.102-10)

6 Why do the Mistress sonnets begin with beauty

We have seen that the fourteen increase sonnets, which begin the male sequence, are preoccupied with preserving physical beauty and only mention truth in the last few lines of sonnet 14? How do they relate to sonnets 127 to 137 that begin the female sequence as the only other group of sonnets that focus exclusively on beauty and similarly mention truth in the last few lines of sonnet 137?

So far we have surveyed the landscape of the 154 sonnets by first taking note of the overall givens of nature and female/male Shakespeare structures into the whole set and its two sequences. Then, as we begin to engage with the sonnets themselves, we hear Shakespeare present us with a logical argument about the biological implications of the division of male from female in nature. He argues that the division of male from the originary female is the precursor for 'increase' and hence 'love'.

As we work our way through the first fourteen sonnets, we hear that 'love' is biologically dependent on 'increase'. Then, to add to the preconditions, we find in sonnet 14 that if increase is not acknowledged then 'truth and beauty' is doomed.

So, just what is 'truth and beauty'?

Our scrutiny of the sonnet set informs us that the words truth and beauty are mentioned in both sequences. In the Master Mistress sequence we find that only beauty is mentioned until sonnet 14 with truth being introduced in its last few lines. Then 'truth and beauty' are intermixed frequently throughout the remaining Master Mistress sonnets from 15 to 126.

In particular, after truth and beauty occur together in sonnets 14 and 17, they occur together in a further seven sonnets (37, 41, 54, 60, 62, 69, 101) and follow one another in some pairs of sonnets (66/67, 69/70, 95/96). Otherwise they are scattered individually throughout a further twenty two sonnets. We also notice that in a few cases truth and/or beauty is followed by a sonnet that harks back to the increase sonnets (95/96/97).

Significantly, truth and beauty are configured differently in the Mistress sequence. Shakespeare quite deliberately separates them so that only beauty is mentioned in the first eleven sonnets to the female (127 to the beginning of 137) and only truth is mentioned in the following sonnets (from the end of 137 until 152). No other love poet of Shakespeare's day – or before and since – singles out beauty and then truth for such focused treatment.

Shakespeare's separation of beauty from truth in the Mistress sequence is so decisive it deserves investigation. If we add the unity evident in the numbering of the 28 Mistress sonnets to the intriguing separation of beauty and truth in sonnets 127 to 152, we are lead to consider the final 28 sonnets first.

We note that, despite the word beauty predominating until the first mention of truth at the end of sonnet 137, a dedicated increase argument does not occur anywhere in the Mistress' 28 sonnets. While some sonnets such as 135/136 and 146 mention 'store' – Shakespeare's synonym for increase introduced in sonnet 14 – it is not the primary focus of the sequence. After all, the female is the prior entity so she is the source of increase.

Instead, it is the final pair of sonnets, 153 and 154, that stand out. But they catch the eye for the opposite reason, it seems, from the fourteen increase sonnets. Whereas the increase sonnets are very literal and argumentative in tone, sonnets 153 and 154 are very metaphorical and decidedly erotic. If we can account for the change from the fourteen sonnets at the beginning of the set to the two sonnets at the end we may be some way towards understanding Shakespearean love.

Further scans reveal the Mistress sequence does not examine specifically the idea of writing or poetry or art. And, for that matter, 'time' is absent as is the Christian God[32], although both appear in the Master Mistress sonnets. Yet the female or Mistress evinces a unity, a reality and a maturity in love not apparent in the Poet's often critical attitude to the 'self love' of the male or Master Mistress.

Moving closer we see the discussion about beauty in the first eleven Mistress sonnets seems much more focused on the philosophic implications of the word beauty than were the increase sonnets where beauty is more a physical attribute. In the Mistress sonnets beauty is used to refer to all sensory inputs and their impact on the human mind. Shakespeare's Poet seems to be taking a lesson in sensory effects from a Mistress who will not be cowered by idealised conventions of beauty as she prepares him for a maturity in love.

Appropriately, we find sonnets 127, 128, 130, 131, 132, 137 consider incoming or unmediated sensations impinging on the external sense organs that affect the Poet's mind as he observes the Mistress in her natural/social environment. While the eye is the archetypal sensory organ that represents all the senses throughout the sonnets, sonnet 130 includes three other senses as well[33].

---

[32] *The three mentions of the word 'God' in the sonnets are quite distinctive. The first, in sonnet 58, seems like a reference to the Christian male God:*

> **That God forbid,** that made me first your slave, (*sonnet 58, 1*)

The second, in sonnet 110, seems to refer to a more accommodating God such as the Roman God Jupiter or Jove – who appears in the plays a number of times:

> **A God in love,** to whom I am confined. (*sonnet 110, 12*)

And the third, in sonnet 154, invokes Cupid (from sonnet 153), the God of love:

> **The little Love-God** lying once asleep, (*sonnet 154, 1*)

The shift up from the dominating male-God of the Bible, to the 'shower of gold' Jupiter, to the Roman God dedicated to love-making, highlights Shakespeare's critique of unloving God-based power – epitomised by the God-dependent Richard III.

[33] *Sonnet 130 first itemises the sense of sight:*

> My Mistress' **eyes** are nothing like the Sun,
> Coral is far more red, than her lips red,

Then the sense of smell:

> And in some **perfumes** is there more delight,
> Than in the breath that from my Mistress reeks.

Then the sense of hearing:

> I love to **hear her speak,** yet well I know,
> That Music hath a far more pleasing sound:

Then the sense of touch:

> I grant I never saw a goddess go,
> My Mistress **when she walks treads on the ground**. (*sonnet 130, 1-12*)

As we listen, we hear Shakespeare use the word 'beauty' quite definitely to refer to any incoming sensation whether it is later deemed fair or foul. His Poet argues in sonnet 127, which mentions 'beauty' or 'beauty's' six times, that calling a sensation fair or foul is a stylistic judgment made consequent upon sensory input[34]. The Poet continues the investigation of the archetypal sense of sight in sonnets 131 and 132 and brings it to a conclusion in the first part of sonnet 137.

Before we see what sonnet 137 has to say about beauty, there are two sonnets between 127 and 137 that stand somewhat apart. Sonnet 128 has a double role in the set of sonnets. It both plays with the sense of touch as part of the investigation of 'beauty' and, in concert with sonnet 8, mentions music twice in its first line indicating its part in a music pattern woven into the set[35]. As both 'music/music' sonnets occur in parts of the set in which only sensory beauty is mentioned, Shakespeare second-strings music into the developmental stages toward mature love.

Sonnet 129 – along with its companion sonnet 146 in the truth group – sounds a different note. Both sonnets act as lightning rods to show how the natural logic of the sonnet set, hinted at in the biblical criticism apparent in sonnets like 127, arcs over to the social/political/religious critique basic to the plays. They reveal the sonnets to be a double act, both pertinent to interpersonal love/hate and relevant to religious/social love/hate.

Then, there is another dimension inherent in the nature/female/male structure of the set. As indicated earlier, the generic characters in the 154 sonnets are both female and male persons who interrelate in the world and feminine and masculine personae active in any human mind. Hence in sonnets 133 and 134 we find the Poet includes the male as Master Mistress in his assessment of sensory input. The Poet emphasises that – just as much as persons in love – the feminine and masculine personae of a loving mind need to be logically aligned with the dynamic of incoming sensations.

---

[34] *Sonnet 127 quite specifically identifies an 'age' when the logic of 'beauty' was not corrupted by male-based 'Creation'. It says a 'bastard shame' has adopted or 'put on Nature's power' denigrating women with 'Art's false borrowed face'. For the Poet to experience mature love he first needs to understand how the natural senses have been curtailed by 'false esteem' – even if recovering the esteem of natural beauty blasphemously slanders biblical 'Creation' with its 'bastard' or unnatural God-like beauty named 'fair':*

In the **old age** black was not counted fair,
Or if it were it bore not beauty's name:
But now is black beauty's successive heir,
And **Beauty slandered with a bastard shame**,
For since each hand has **put on Nature's power**,
Fairing the foul with **Art's false borrowed face**,
Sweet beauty hath no name no holy bower,
But **is profaned, if not lives in disgrace**.
Therefore my Mistress' eyes are Raven black,
Her eyes so suited, and they mourners seem,
At such who not born fair no beauty lack,
Slandering Creation with a false esteem, (*sonnet 127*, 1-12)

[35] *The patterns for music along with those for time are discussed in 'WSSP'.*

The way Shakespeare incorporates the music sonnets, 8 and 128, the personae sonnets 133/134 (including, as we will see, sonnets 41/42 and 143/144), and sonnets 129 and 146 into his more basic treatment of 'beauty' and 'truth' and 'truth and beauty' provides a measure of his natural ability to incorporate a complex of ideas into such a simple and natural pattern based in nature and the sexual dynamic. He shows by example how it is possible to inter-relate the many facets of human understanding in a set of philosophic poetry.

The two distinctive sonnets, 135 and 136, that come just before the transitional sonnet 137, anticipate with considerable verve and humour the sonnets from 138 onward in which the Mistress and Poet talk together for the first time in the set. Sonnets 135 and 136 identify the singular moment when a sensation entering the mind is first named to provide the grammar of language with its potential to generate meaning. In this case the Mistress' 'love' is identified with the 'one' who physically experiences her 'treasure' – the eponymously named 'Will'[36].

And Shakespeare's legendary grasp of language is on show as he displays the various meanings of 'Will' in sonnets 135 and 136. By playing erotically with the name 'Will', with its interrelated meanings of penis and human intent, Shakespeare mimics the way language is modeled on the richness of the female/male dynamic in nature[37]. Both sonnets 135 and 136 celebrate the crossover from the unity of the female and the singular moment of 'store' or increase that leads to the infinite variety of human types to the suggestive possibilities associated with naming ever-mercurial sensations.

The Poet confirms his use of the word 'beauty' as an inclusive term for all incoming sensations in the first four lines of sonnet 137. He argues that such

---

[36] *If sonnet 136 – along with 135 – were written in the period when the sonnets set was being finalised, they show a Shakespeare reveling in the relationship of nature, the sexual dynamic, increase, numbering, sensations and naming liberated from the conventions and compromises of male-based beliefs:*

> *Will*, will fulfill the treasure of thy love,
> I fill it full with **wills**, and **my will one**,
> In things of great receipt with ease we prove,
> Among a **number one** is reckon'd none.
> Then in the **number** let me pass untold,
> Though in **thy store's account** I one must be,
> For **nothing** hold me so it please thee hold,
> That **nothing** me, a **some-thing** sweet to thee.
> **Make but my name thy love, and love that still,**
> **And then thou lovest me for my name is** *Will. (sonnet 136, 5-14)*

[37] *Shakespeare's appreciation of the logic of language shows in his mastery of punning dialogue in his poems and plays. He anticipates Wittgenstein's explanation of the way the unmediated sensation of pain becomes verbalized as 'ouch' and then named as part of the language game of pain. But, as is typical of Shakespeare's exploitation of the grammar of words, he appreciates that the same word has different shades of meaning to the degree that his nature-based neologisms have proved so enduring. Shakespeare's lexiconic edge arises because he locates the logic of language unequivocally in his nature-based philosophy with the female/male dynamic giving his understanding of love a depth the more tentative Wittgenstein could not begin to match.*

sensations on their own are quite indiscriminate as measures of what is 'best' and what is 'worst'. Sonnet 137 states that the 'blind fool love' cannot rely on 'eyes' falsehood' to satisfy the 'judgment of my heart'[38]. The eyes alone cannot be a measure of falsehood, as they may be for purely sensate beings, because human nature has learnt to rely on judgment through language to adjudicate true and false.

If Shakespeare grounds the complete set of 154 sonnets and its two sequences in nature and the sexual dynamic of female and male – with the proviso of the increase argument provided in sonnets 1 to 14 – then in the first 11 Mistress sonnets he prepares the groundwork for the moment in nature that human beings become preeminently conscious of their surroundings through their senses.

It seems that Shakespeare, through his Poet, begins his presentation of the mind's potentiality and the human capacity for love by first accounting, like any good philosopher, for the way in which humans become cognizant of the world about them – through the senses. If, as Shakespeare seems to argue, the deep experience of love is inured in the human sensibility because of the natural relation of female and male, then love's means of connecting female to male, female to female and male to male in the world about, is through unmediated sensory effects on the mind.

As we have seen, to make his point, while the Poet addresses primarily the sensory effects of the female on his sense organs, he includes the male in sonnets 133 and 134 to emphasise the significance of the sexual dynamic and increase as grounds for the continuing capacity to receive sensations. The double interrelationship between female/male persons in sonnet 133 and feminine/masculine personae in sonnet 134 rounds out the natural dynamic that devolves from the givens of the set[39] – as will become more apparent as we proceed.

We will see that the spoken and written language in which the intimations of the 'heart' (sonnet 137) are expressed and understood is central to Shakespeare's ability to convey the experience of mature love.

Shakespeare divides the Mistress sequence into three groups with the first group from sonnet 127 to the beginning of sonnet 137 presenting the logic of incoming sensations

---

[38] *Sonnet 137 exemplifies the role some sonnets play as transitional zones between two aspects of Shakespeare's philosophy. It first summarises what the Poet means by beauty:*
Thou blind fool love, what dost thou to **mine eyes**,
That they behold and see not what they see:
They **know what beauty is, see where it lies**,
Yet what the best is, take the worst to be: (*sonnet 137*, 1-4)

[39] *In sonnet 133 the relationship is between the Poet and the youth as a 'friend':*
Beshrew that heart that makes my heart to groan,
For that deep wound it gives **my friend and me**;
I'st not enough to torture me alone,
But slave to slavery my sweet'st friend must be. (*sonnet 133*, 1-4)
And in sonnet 134 the relationship is of the Poet to his youthful self:
So now I have confessed that he is thine,
And I my self am mortgaged to thy will,
Myself I'll forfeit, so **that other mine**,
Thou wilt restore to be my comfort still: (*sonnet 134*, 1-4)

or beauty. When Shakespeare uses the word 'beauty' to identify incoming sensations as singular effects, he prepares the mind for his development of a consistent appreciation of mature love.

7 Why truth follows beauty when the Mistress and Poet first talk of love

Shakespeare is unique in having the incoming senses (beauty) and mind-based language (truth) treated so separately and so deliberately in a set of love sonnets. So what happens when he takes us from the indiscriminateness of sensory love to verbalized love whose veracity can be sworn and forsworn as happens when the Mistress and Poet first talk of their love in sonnet 138?

Shakespeare explores the logic of 'truth' from the latter part of sonnet 137 through to sonnet 152. In keeping with the focus on 'truth', the word 'beauty' is completely absent from the truth group. Instead, to emphasise the significance of truth, sonnets 138 and 152 at the beginning and end of the group mention the word 'truth' twice.

'Truth' according to the last few lines of sonnet 137 is the dynamic of saying. It is when we 'say' something that we discriminate consciously between one sensation and another[40]. Moreover, because a grasp of the logic of language is vital to the Poet's experience and expression of mature love, the word 'love' is mentioned in all the Mistress sonnets in which truth is active except sonnets 143 and 146 for reasons that will become apparent.

By naming a particular sensation (remember sonnets 135 and 136) in the context of saying we establish a convention in which the sensation is identified with that name, in effect making it 'true' to that name[41]. Significantly, all other sensations are defined as 'false' to that name so establishing the basis for predictably assigning true and false – at least more predictable than relying on sensations. Sonnet 138 explains just how this dynamic of true and false works in practice.

So, when we listen to sonnet 138 – with 'truth' twice – the Poet has the Mistress say something for the first time in her sequence. She 'swears' she is made of 'truth' and it is the process of swearing that provides the clue to the role of language in giving voice to the sensory intimations of love between willing human beings[42].

If we look back to sonnet 131, we hear that the Poet swears to himself 'alone'[43]. Shakespeare recognises perceptively that swearing alone is not swearing

---

[40] *Toward the end of sonnet 137 the Poet prepares the reader for the following sonnets from 138 to 152 that focus on the meaning of 'truth' as Shakespeare uses it:*
   Or **mine eyes seeing this, say this is not**
   To put fair **truth** upon so foul a face. (*sonnet 137, 11-12*)

[41] *As we unravel Shakespeare's philosophy we can see that the empowering context for saying is the sexual dynamic in nature. Wittgenstein recognised this in part when he said the relationships within language games could be compared to 'family resemblances' and talked of 'natural history' and the fact of 'parents' as the unquestionable grounds for language.*

[42] *The first line of sonnet 138 could not be more explicit in heralding its intent to lay down the logic of language:*
   When **my love swears that she is made of truth**, (*sonnet 138, 1*)

[43] *Sonnet 131, from the group of Mistress sonnets that present the logic of 'beauty', shows*

at all because swearing involves an agreement between two or more language using respondents. So, amidst the Mistress sonnets that consider beauty or immediate sensations, Shakespeare both recognises 'beauty' as an unarticulated prelude to verbalised awareness – swearing to oneself – and anticipates the logic of swearing from sonnet 138 onwards that the conceit of a private swearing to oneself presumes on grammatically and hence logically.

As the give and take between the Mistress and the Poet in sonnet 138 exemplifies, words are mere bearers of the content of the speaker's intent. It is possible to say the opposite of what you mean yet still convey what you intend[44]. So someone can say they love a person yet not mean it, just as it is possible for someone to say they do not love a person yet the person hears loud and clear of their undying love. And Shakespeare the consummate dramatist knows it all depends on the internal and external stage settings[45].

Shakespeare's philosophic acuity. He is supremely conscious that when he describes the effects of 'beauty' he uses language to convey his thoughts:
> Although **I swear it to my self alone.**
> And **to be sure that is not false I swear**
> A thousand groans but thinking on thy face,
> One on another's neck do witness bear
> **Thy black is fairest in my judgments place.** (*sonnet 131*, 8-12)

[44] *The sensitivity of the Mistress to the logic of language in sonnet 138 is garnered through her intimate understanding of the derivation of the dynamic of sensations and ideas from the sexual dynamic in nature. In the couplet the Poet expresses the insight by conflating sexual intimacy and intellectual give and take:*
> **I do believe her though I know she lies,**
> That she might think me some untutored youth,
> Unlearned in the world's false subtleties.
> Thus vainly thinking that she thinks me young,
> Although she knows my days are past the best,
> **Simply I credit her false speaking tongue,**
> On both sides thus is simple truth suppressed:
> But wherefore says she not she is unjust?
> And wherefore say not I that I am old?
> O love's best habit is in seeming trust,
> And age in love, loves not t'have years told.
> **Therefore I lie with her, and she with me,**
> **And in our faults by lies we flattered be.** (*sonnet 138*, 2-14)

[45] *Iago's use of the capacity of language to represent or misrepresent intentions in 'Othello' is the most vivid example of Shakespeare's insight into the logic of human discourse. Othello reveals his lack of mind-based maturity when he fails to anticipate 'honest' Iago's deceit. That Iago does understand how language can deceive reveals just how basic Shakespeare considers a clear appreciation of the logic of 'truth' or language to be. Othello's ultimate conceit shared by most of Shakespeare's audience then and now is to believe in the 'lie' of a creator God external to the imagining human mind and make that lie the centre-piece of a religio-political system. The false belief corrupts language at its nature-based core and sets the scene for all the Iago-like consequences of religious inquisition and atrocities – particularly in witch hunts and stake-burnings against*

By basing his sonnet set in nature and the female/male dynamic, Shakespeare provides a sound grounding for the agreed conventions of language. He both appreciates the logic of naming as crucial to determining sense (true and false) and that naming is an arbitrary act that establishes a convention that holds as long as there is agreement to sustain it.

So language or saying (truth) is more contrived and hence more manipulable than the sensory effects (beauty) that impinge on the eyes, ears, tongue, fingers, or nose over which we have no control except to stop them out in unconsciousness. In the sonnets that treat of beauty and then truth we can follow the Poet watching and thinking as he records diligently for our instruction the lessons he has learnt from the Mistress about the basic logic of language as it enhances the input of the senses.

But Shakespeare's intent is even more incisive than just recognizing the logic of language based in sensations. In these famous love sonnets built out of thousands of words according to the grammar of propositions and poetry to excite both reason and emotions he is saying that if the logic of language is understood then deeper and more abiding is the love that accrues to the savvy swearer of truth.

We have seen Shakespeare base his understanding of love in nature and the sexual dynamic of female and male and the potential of increase. And we anticipate he will account for our deepest emotions because his poetry incites those emotions in us. Now we find sonnet 138 says quite explicitly that love is mature only for those who understand the logic of language. The verbal jousting between Poet and Mistress does not lead to heated argument and strife because they both understand the power as well as the limitation of words.

We can see Shakespeare demonstrating his insight into the dynamic of language in many of his plays when characters who are at odds – or not yet accommodated to one another – suddenly trip the switch that enables them to communicate with ease regardless of what is said or not said. In *Measure for Measure* Vincentio and Isabella have just such an epiphany, in *Twelfth Night* Feste teaches Orsino the logic of language which prepares him for a relationship with the canny Viola, in *Much Ado About Nothing* Beatrice and Benedick talk past each other until they hear one another and in *The Taming of the Shrew* Petruchio forces Katherine to appreciate the conventional logic of language so that by the play's end she can avow with consummate tongue-in-cheekiness undying obedience to him.[46]

---

women. Shakespeare signals the impending doom for both Othello and Desdemona's failed attempt to extricate themselves from the Venetian God-based patriarchy of her father by injecting 'hell' and 'demon' into their names.

[46] *Petruchio first expresses his insight that Kate's head needs sorting:*
   Petruchio: And thus I'll curb **her mad and headstrong humour**:
   He that knows better how to tame a shrew,
   Now let him speak, *(The Taming of the Shrew, 3.3.1843-5)*
   Then a little later, Petruchio shows Kate how to break free of the tyranny of language where words presume mastery over the things they name – just as the name God is imposed on nature without mercy:
   Petruchio: I say it is the **Moon**.
   Kate: I know it is the **Moon**.

In the tragedies the opposite is the case. Othello and Desdemona have not achieved the accommodation of sonnet 138, nor has Hamlet in his play, and the love-struck Romeo and Juliet are kept from maturing their natural verbal allegiance by the interference of their parents whose language is corrupted by male-based custom and habit.

All the plays demonstrate that Shakespearean love requires an easy familiarity with the logic of words – otherwise stage-worthy comedy or tragedy ensues. The misunderstanding by Shakespearean critics of the critical moments of insight and disaster in the plays shows just how universally language has been converted away from the service of natural love. Commentators fail to hear the moment in *Measure for Measure*, for instance, when novice nun Isabella and Duke Vincentio find engaging love because they reach a marriage of true minds[47].

> *Petruchio*: Nay then you lie: it is the **blessed Sun**.
> *Kate*: Then **God** be blest, it is the **blessed sun**,
> But **sun** it is not, when you say it is not.
> And the **Moon** changes even as your mind:
> **What you will have it named, even that it is,** (*The Taming of the Shrew*,
> 4.3.2315-8)
>
> *Kate appropriately implicates 'God' in the dissembling she has been subjected to by her paternalistic father.*

[47] *When Isabella argues it is 'most strange' that Angelo is not only 'forsworn' but 'a murderer', 'an adulterous thief', 'an hypocrite' and a 'virgin violator', Duke Vincentio agrees 'it is ten times strange'. (Measure for Measure, 5.1.2391-2397)*

At this point Isabella responds lamely with the idealistic misconception that truth is eternal:

> *Isabella*: It is not truer he is Angelo,
> Than this is all as true, as it is strange:
> Nay, it is ten times true, **for truth is truth**
> **To th'end of reck'ning**. (*Measure for Measure*, 5.1.2398-2401)

Because Isabella cannot see that the logic of truth is a dynamic of true and false, Vincentio accuses her of 'infirmity of sense'. But then she corrects herself and rejects Angelo for being 'absolute' and talks of truth as a process in which the relation between the true and the false is weighed:

> *Isabella*: Oh gracious Duke
> Harp not on that; nor do not banish reason
> For inequality, **but let your reason serve**
> **To make the truth appear, where it seems hid,**
> **And hide the false seems true.** (*Measure for Measure*, 5.1.2421-5)

Vincentio then commends her patent sanity:

> *Vincentio*: **Many that are not mad**
> **Have sure more lack of reason:** (*Measure for Measure*, 5.1.2426-7)

The relationship between the Vincentio and Isabella has developed to the stage where they are able to employ the logic of 'truth' in unison. If the singular beauty of the novice nun originally took Vincentio's attention, her newly gained awareness of the idealistic duplicity that affects both Angelo and herself profoundly alters her mind, and aligns her understanding with Vincentio's. This is the moment when Isabella and Vincentio fall naturally in love.

Returning to the Mistress sonnets, we can track the focus on the dynamic of language from sonnet 138 right through to 152. Sonnets 139 and 140 reiterate and explore the implications of the move from the senses ('eyes') to language ('tongue').

Then sonnet 141 refers very explicitly – and humorously – to the relationship between the 'five senses' and the 'five wits'[48]. It reiterates the transition from the 'five senses' to the dynamic of truth or the 'five wits' as Shakespeare calls the cranial looping that is truth. All five senses are mentioned and, by calling the dynamic of saying the 'five wits', his Poet reinforces the logical relationship between the five sensory organs and ideas that develop in the mind.

Sonnet 142 is the first of four sonnets (142, 145, 149 and 150) to examine specifically the logical interrelationship between love and hate. All four argue that love readily turns to hate if the logic of language in nature is not fully understood and implemented. Sonnet 145 talks of the Poet's own experience in which the Mistress shows him how to convert 'hate' to 'love'. And there is every reason to think sonnet 145 celebrates Shakespeare's own moment of insight learnt early on from his lifelong partner and mother of his children, Anne Hathaway[49].

The mature Poet, under the guidance of the Mistress, can now navigate his way through the sea of emotions verbalized as love and hate. By controlling 'love hate'[50], as the Mistress does in sonnet 149, the Poet achieves command of the tendency of language to incite obsessive love or excessive hate when divorced from nature for purely mind-based ends.

As sonnet 150 reveals, if the Mistress is misogynistically an object of hate, the Poet learns to love her because the dichotomies of language were not intended to create difference but to enable effective representation of one thing distinct from

---

[48] *As is Shakespeare's practice, sonnet 141 looks back to the beauty of the five senses and reinforces the current concern with truth or the five wits:*
> In faith I do not love thee with **mine eyes,**
>
> …
>
> Nor are **mine ears** with thy tongue's tune delighted,
> Nor **tender feeling to base touches** prone,
> Nor **taste**, nor **smell**, desire to be invited
> To any sensual feast with thee alone:
> But **my five wits**, nor **my five senses** can
> Dissuade one foolish heart from serving thee, (*sonnet 141*, 1-10)

[49] *The pun in the couplet of sonnet 145 on 'hate away' and 'and', and the identification of the Poet's name as 'Will' in sonnet 136, suggests Shakespeare learnt the dynamic of hate and love from his wife Anne Hathaway:*
> I hate, from **hate away** she threw,
> **And** saved my life saying not you. (*sonnet 145*, 13-14)

In 'Shakespeare's Wife', Germaine Greer argues that Anne Hathaway would have managed their combined household and business affairs competently and may have played a part in preparing the 1623 Folio for publication as she died that year. (Germaine Greer, *Shakespeare's Wife*, London, Bloomsbury, 2007)

[50] *Sonnet 149 adjoins the words' love hate' to show their intimate relatedness:*
> But **love hate** on for now I know thy mind,
> Those that can see thou lov'st, and I am blind. (*sonnet 149*, 13-14)

another analogous to the way the female is the foil for the male in the dynamic of increase[51].

Sonnet 145 is particularly poignant because in it the Poet relives his hard-won education under the tutelage of the Mistress from the syndrome of hate until he achieves the insight to love the Mistress as an equal. We will have to explore further the relationship between love and hate if we are to understand Shakespeare's control of the depths of love evident in his sonnets (and plays) – remembering 'self love' equals self hate[52].

Humorously, in sonnet 143 Shakespeare provides a mocking interlude to remind us that the role of the Mistress is to presume on the maturity of those males who have gained maturity while continuing to make immature males aware of the logic of life and love. Sonnet 143, as the first of two sonnets in which the Master Mistress appears in the truth group in the Mistress sequence, parodies the flightiness of immature minds – with the Mistress dealing to both Poet and the male youth.

Sonnet 144 is a direct attack on the illogical consequences of instituting a male God over nature. The Poet laments that his 'two loves' in which the male is suppos-edly 'right fair' and the female a 'worser spirit' are in a twist of corruption and purity that will not be resolved until the supposed bad angel (the woman) fires the good angel (the male) from his usurped priority[53]. Love, for Shakespeare, cannot exist with contentedness until the natural priorities of female and male are recovered.

And, as we have noted, along with sonnet 129, sonnet 146 stands somewhat apart. Its function appears both pertinent to the argument of the set and extends the natural logic of the 154-sonnet set to the social/political/religious critiques of the plays.

Then we hear sonnets 147 and 148 examine aspects of the language dynamic.

---

[51] *Sonnet 150 reiterates the lesson the Poet recounts in sonnet 145:*
Who taught thee how to make me love thee more,
The more I hear and see just cause of hate,
Oh **though I love what others do abhor,**
With others thou shouldst not abhor my state.
If thy unworthiness raised love in me,
More worthy I to be beloved of thee. (*sonnet 150*, 9-14)

[52] *Here, by the evidence of the sonnets and plays, is the reason why the male God as the great self-loved so readily incites hate.*

[53] *Sonnets 143 and 144 from the truth group inter-relate Mistress, Master Mistress and Poet as do sonnets 133 and 134 in the beauty group. Sonnet 143 treats the three protagonists as persons and sonnet 144 carries out a mock exorcism as if they are religiously confused mind-based personae. In contrast to sonnets 133 and 134 where the sensory impact of the 'cruel eye' and 'beauty' are considered, sonnet 144 contrasts two states of mind where the conscious 'wooing' of supposed 'purity' by 'foul pride' leads to a resolution of the illogicalities of male/female imbalance:*
But being **both from me both to each friend,**
I guess one angel in an other's hell.
Yet this shall I ne'er know but live in doubt,
Till my bad angel fire my good one out. (*sonnet 144*, 11-14)

In sonnet 147 the Poet challenges the dictate of 'Reason' or language that separates fair from dark when he knows that his 'black as hell' Mistress is 'fair' despite the dogmatic conventions of traditional religions that conceal their constitutional misogyny behind disingenuous heavenly love. Sonnet 148 turns the situation around with the Poet assuming wittily the role of the love-struck idealist whose 'judgment is fled' leaving him susceptible to the 'cunning' – hear cunt – of the Mistress and so condemning her when he should condemn his own idealistic love[54].

Sonnet 151 reiterates the natural inter-relationship of 'conscience', or the effects of the language operation on the mind, and 'love'[55], or the implications of the increase dynamic established in sonnet 9. As the penultimate truth sonnet in the Mistress sequence it both looks back to the source of love and conscience in the increase sonnets and, with its wonderful erotic suggestiveness looks forward to the role of the highly erotic sonnets 153 and 154[56]. We will see later how this form of eroticism is basic to expressing Shakespearean love.

Sonnet 152 ends the lesson in the truth dynamic with a flourish of truth words such as swearing, forswearing, vowing, oaths, etc[57]. It repeats the insight,

[54] *In sonnet 148 Shakespeare continues winding up the erotic innuendo before the triumph of sonnets 153 and 154:*
> **O cunning love**, with tears thou keepst me blind,
> **Lest eyes well seeing thy foul faults should find**. (*sonnet 148, 13,14*)

[55] *Sonnet 151 begins by reiterating the significance between the logic of increase for love and the sense of right and wrong that develops naturally in the human mind as a consequence:*
> **Love** is too young to know what **conscience** is,
> Yet who knows not **conscience is born of love**, (*sonnet 151, 1-2*)

[56] *In sonnet 151 Shakespeare uses eroticism to give expression to the derivation of language from the sexual dynamic:*
> But **rising at thy name doth point out thee**,
> As his triumphant prize, **proud of this pride**,
> He is contented thy poor drudge to be
> To **stand in thy affairs, fall by thy side**.
> No want of **conscience** hold it that I call,
> Her love, **for whose dear love I rise and fall**. (*sonnet 151, 9-14*)

[57] *There could hardly be a more forthright demonstration of the logic of truth than that which Shakespeare's Poet gives in the final truth sonnet in the Mistress sequence. Sonnet 152 is loaded with the dynamic of 'simple truth' as it counters the illogicality of truth called 'simplicity' – as we will see in sonnet 66:*
> In loving thee thou know'st I am **forsworn**,
> But thou art **twice forsworn** to me love **swearing**,
> In act thy **bed-vow broke** and **new faith torn**,
> In **vowing new hate** after new love bearing:
> But why of **two oaths breach** do I accuse thee,
> When I break twenty: I am **perjured** most,
> For all my **vows** are **oaths** but to misuse thee:
> And all my **honest faith** in thee is lost.

illustrated in sonnet 138, that a truth sworn or a vow taken can just as readily be forsworn or broken[58]. Shakespeare could hardly be more explicit in showing how the dynamic of 'truth' functions as the give and take in language. By associating a broken 'bed-vow' with a 'faith torn' he reiterates the logical relation between female and male and the dynamic of truth in the mind.

As we have traversed the Mistress sonnets through beauty and then truth, we have seen that the love the Poet feels in his heart is not anchored in beauty or truth but in their rootedness in nature. Getting the expression of love in the language of poetry right is only possible when its natural groundedness frees the effects of sensory input expressed in language from the prejudices of fashion and the worship of the word. The Poet has been taught by the Mistress how 'truth' functions in nature.

Shakespeare follows the group of Mistress sonnets devoted solely to beauty with the group of sonnets from the end of 137 to 152 devoted solely to truth or the use of language. Clarity about using language to swear and forswear between true and false because language mimics the female/male dynamic in nature ensures the necessary intentionality for understanding and expressing Shakespearean love.

For I have **sworn deep oaths** of thy deep kindness:
Oaths of thy love, thy **truth**, thy constancy,
And to enlighten thee gave eyes to blindness,
Or made them **swear** against the thing they see.
For I have **sworn** thee fair: more **perjured** eye,
To swear against the truth so foul a lie. (*sonnet 152*)

[58] *In Shakespeare's understanding of 'truth' there is an appreciation of the logic of language that predates Ludwig Wittgenstein by 350 years. Wittgenstein came to understand that language use is based in conventions that are formed according to the prevailing conditions but when those conditions change the language game changes and this happens continuously in human intercourse. But Wittgenstein also realised that the shifting conventions of language always leave 'nature' and the need for 'parents' untouched. Similarly, Shakespeare appreciates that the logic of language, in which sworn oaths are readily forsworn, is based in the natural dynamic female/male. But, because he gives his understanding unconditional expression in terms of the female/male dynamic in nature, his presentation is extraordinarily more vivid than Wittgenstein's and capable of evoking the profoundest human love. Unlike Wittgenstein, Shakespeare's superior philosophy enables him to distinguish clearly between 'truth' of language as ethics and 'beauty' or any form of sensation as aesthetics. No wonder Wittgenstein was at a loss to appreciate just what made Shakespeare's works so attractive to others while he remained unable to plumb their greatness. His continued commitment to the formalities of religion and his doubts over the explanatory power of Darwin's theory of evolution crippled his otherwise lucid insights into the logic of language.*

8 Love of writing and writing of love

How can Shakespeare presume to write a set of love sonnets that begin with the need to accept the significance of 'increase' if the biology of increase is a precondition for the act of writing as well as for 'love'? Or, how can Shakespeare say what he says about nature and the sexual dynamic when they are the givens for saying?

Because they are so different in style, if not in content, we will leave the final two sonnets 153 and 154 until after our investigation into the implications for mature love in the Master Mistress sonnets after sonnet 14. We will follow the trail of observations about the status of 'beauty' and then 'truth' in the female sequence back into the early sonnets of the male sequence in which the concepts 'truth and beauty' were first encountered.

We have seen that Shakespeare writes about increase and its implications for love in the first fourteen sonnets yet, when we check, he does not refer reflexively to the process of writing in those sonnets or for that matter in the twenty-eight Mistress sonnets. It is not until the logically connected sonnets 15/16 in the Master Mistress sequence that he mentions and addresses the effect and effectiveness of writing.

Just previously, in sonnet 14, we heard the Poet tell the youth that if he does not accept the logic of increase or 'store' then forget about 'truth and beauty' – forever. We know the word 'beauty' occurs 16 times in the increase sonnets before truth is mentioned twice at the end of sonnet 14 and in each case beauty refers to the physical attributes of the male youth.

Because of the predominance of the word beauty and absence of truth until the end of the increase sonnets, the principal issue in the first 14 sonnets is the physical increase of physical attributes. It is evident that the preservation of physical attributes precedes the introduction of the word 'truth' and anticipates the possibility of writing.

Whereas in the Mistress sequence the Poet learns of the logic of beauty – or any form of incoming sensations – by observing her in her familiar environment, in the increase sonnets the Poet begins by appealing to the youth's awareness of his own appearance – as in the 'glass' or mirror of sonnet 3. So, rather than instruct the youth at this early stage in his sequence in the logic of beauty, the Poet utilises the youth's own capacity to see himself in a mirror to incite in him a concern for the fate of humankind if all humans are as self-loving as he[59].

When we examine sonnets 15 to 19 we find the first and last sonnets – 15 and 19 – mention the word 'love' and of the others, the famous sonnet 18 has only an adverbial 'lovely'. If we look closely we can see this is because sonnet 18 has a crucial function of correlating the logic of increase with the potentiality of writing in the well-known line 'when in eternal lines to time thou grow'st'[60]. Both 'lines' of

---

[59] *Shakespeare's target is not so much niggardly individuals but systems of belief in which the logic of increase is rendered sinful while self-love is idealised as a male God while celibacy and patriarchy get a heavenly blessing*

[60] *Sonnet 18, as the penultimate sonnet in the increase to poetry group, exquisitely*

descent and 'lines' of poetry coalesce as the Poet prepares to add words to the flesh of the natural dynamic by putting thoughts on paper to evoke deeply human love in his readers. Poetry only 'lives' as long as humans continue to 'breathe'.

By addressing the relationship between the biological and written 'lines' in the five sonnets immediately after sonnet 14, the Poet addresses the prerequisites for expressing ideas through writing. It is as if Shakespeare acknowledges that his ability to say anything about nature and increase presumes on their existence as givens.

We can see that sonnet 15 begins by first reiterating the increase argument and by playing on the double meaning of 'engraft' – both as a scion and as inscribing. Its companion sonnet 16 reinforces the shift by transacting the move from 'pen(is)' to 'pencil'[61].

In sonnets 17 to 19, the full implications of writing in relation to increase are addressed until the 'lines' of life and 'verse' are clearly differentiated in sonnet 19. Sonnet 17 specifically reiterates the dependence of 'beauty' – as sensation ('eyes') – and 'truth' – tied to the 'tongue' – on 'some child of yours' being 'alive' at some time after the youth has died[62]. Then in sonnet 19, we hear that while poetry can

---

expresses the inter-connection between increase and writing. Its poetic beauty and poignancy is epitomised by the combination of its dual concerns in one line:

When in eternal lines to time thou grow'st,
So long as men can breathe or eyes can see,
So long lives this, and this gives life to thee. (*sonnet 18,* 12-14)

[61] *By convention, sonnet 15 is considered one of the so-called 'marriage sonnets', but its role is to introduce the issue of writing after the injunction regarding truth and beauty at the end of sonnet 14:*

And all in war with Time for love of you
As he takes from you, I **engraft** you new. (*sonnet 15,* 13-14)

Sonnet 16, logically connected to sonnet 15, confirms the new theme of writing and its relation to increase:

So should the lines of life that life repair
Which this (**Time's pencil or my pupil pen**) (*sonnet 16,* 9-10)

[62] *Sonnet 17, as the central sonnet of the increase and poetry group, mentions both beauty and truth. It reiterates the increase argument in its couplet where the Poet says the youth would live twice through increase – in himself and in his child – as well as in the Poet's 'rhyme' or verse. Editors ignorant of the sonnets' intent alter the punctuation of the final line by putting the comma after 'twice':*

If I could write the **beauty of your eyes,**
And in fresh numbers number all your graces,
The age to come would say this Poet lies,
Such heavenly touches ne'er touched earthly faces.
So should my papers (yellowed with their age)
Be scorned, like old men **of less truth than tongue,**
And your true rights be termed a Poet's rage,
And stretched meter of an Antique song.
But were some child of yours alive that time,
You should live twice in it, and in my rhyme. (*sonnet 17,* 5-14)

indeed capture the beauty of youth at a moment in time, increase perpetuates the full potential of his life[63].

In these five transitional sonnets, Shakespeare acknowledges that the dynamic of increase and the basis for love associated with it are independent of the act of writing. He recognises that his increase sonnets are mere words written on wood pulp and rag made into paper about a physical process that has perpetuated humankind for millions of generations[64] and has the capacity to perpetuate the youth's 'beauty' for many more.

So, as the Poet evokes the increase dynamic and its associated sensations in writing, he reminds us that his words are not made of flesh. Hence the five sonnets 15 to 19 provide the conditional upon which the Poet discusses increase and sensory love and then proceeds to develop his case about the full depth of human love in terms of truth and beauty.

It is evident throughout the sonnets and plays that Shakespeare enjoys immensely the irony of basing his appreciation of the deepest human love in nature and increase[65]. He contrasts his willingness to offer the prerequisites of sonnets 15 to 19, which alert the reader to the difference between writing about love and the physical act of love, with the biblical scribes who refuse to acknowledge they write about an imaginary God.

Yet, the only external evidence of 'God's' imaginary existence, and here is the irony, is in the scribes act of writing. Hence, we can see why believers give excessive value to their sacred books. We will see that Shakespeare's response to a God who has no existence if his books are destroyed, is to write so that the natural 'contents' of his love sonnets can be experienced independently of his book once his nature-based philosophy is understood[66].

---

[63] *Sonnet 19 leaves no doubt that being remembered in verse merely captures the youth at a moment in time compared to the generational benefits of increase. The intensity of love associated with writing is not as elemental as that based in increase. Both forms of love, though, are required for the development of mature love:*

> Yet do thy worst old Time despite thy wrong,
> **My love shall in my verse ever live young.** (*sonnet 19*, 13-14)

[64] *The seeming exaggeration in sonnet 53, where the mention of 'millions' is seen by commentators as hyperbole, is no more than Shakespeare's understanding that there have been millions of generations of human beings:*

> What is your substance, whereof are you made,
> That **millions of strange shadows** on you tend? (*sonnet 53*, 1-2)

[65] *Viola in 'Twelfth Night' argues for Shakespeare's appreciation of the roots of love in increase as she tries to talk Olivia out of her self-imploding idealism:*

> Tis **beauty truly blent**, whose red and white,
> **Nature's own sweet, and cunning hand laid on:**
> Lady, you are the cruel'st she alive,
> If **you will lead these graces to the grave,**
> **And leave the world no copy.** (*Twelfth Night*, 1.5.530-4)

[66] *We will see that Shakespeare argues further that God's scribes neuter him sexually, so creating an erotic entity as sexually impotent as their writing on paper. The self-love that is*

So, as the Poet sets the scene to launch into the remaining Master Mistress sonnets, we might expect him to fulfill our expectation as to the fame of these love sonnets. He has first located the natural logic of love in relation to the biological dynamic of increase and then related the possibility of writing to the increase dynamic. It is as if he is saying the sexual dynamic of female and male in nature is the logical basis for the possibility of love and writing.

To this point, Shakespeare's biologically grounded 'love' may seem incompatible with the deep and abiding idealistically sublime love or the romantically immediate love for which some of the sonnets are resorted to so fervently. Love based in the sexual dynamic of female and male and increase may appear to many readers as no more than a form of animal love hardly commensurate with the human capacity for deeply spiritual love, romantic love and the cathartic expression of love in poetry or art.

Near universally, the first nineteen or so sonnets have been denigrated as sonnets for hire in the cause of marriage because their function in establishing precursors for love has not been appreciated[67]. But if we are diligent we might accept in the interim that Shakespeare is merely identifying Darwin-like the grounds upon which the deepest human love is founded[68].

Shakespeare accounts for our ability to transmit ideas through poetry or any form of writing in the five sonnets from 15 to 19. Appreciating the dependence of poetry or writing on the increase dynamic in nature to ensure the use of words and images is meaningful provides the level of reflexivity required for articulating Shakespearean love.

---

the male God contradicts the significance of increase in nature proving such self-love has its genesis solely in the mind. We will see the consequences of the conceit or inversion of nature as we follow Shakespeare deeper into his love sonnets.

[67] *Ted Hughes, for instance, despite intuiting the primacy of the female for Shakespeare's poems and plays in 'Shakespeare and the Goddess of Complete Being', dismisses the increase sonnets as 'persuasions of hired labour', and in his determination that sonnets 116 and 129 are the key to understanding the whole set (they supposedly contrast ideal love and excessive lust) he ignores the role of the Poet in establishing the emotional and intellectual requirements for mature love based on an acceptance of nature and the sexual dynamic as givens.* (Ted Hughes, *Shakespeare and the Goddess of Complete Being*, Faber and Faber, London, 1992.)

[68] *In 'Darwin's Lost Theory of Love', David Loye shows that in 'The Descent of Man' Darwin applies his earlier theories of prehuman evolution from 'The Origin of Species' to humankind. But Darwin argues that our 'mental powers' and 'moral sense' including the capacity to 'love' – a word he mentions ninety five times – is more significant in human evolution than the 'survival of the fittest' – which he only mentions twice. Loye reveals a Darwin whose understanding of evolutionary significance of human emotions and morality is ironically overlooked in the pre-human determinism of neo-Darwinists who base their speculation principally on 'The Origin of Species'. Classic is Richard Dawkins' unintentionally self-parodying theory of the selfish gene.* (David Loye, *Darwin's Lost Theory of Love*, Lincoln, toExcel, 2000.)

9 Establishing the status of the Master Mistress and the pattern of truth and beauty in his sequence

As Shakespeare leads us deeper into the Master Mistress sequence, in the sonnet pair 20/21 he first reiterates the biological relationship of female to male in nature that grounds the 154-sonnet set to provide the basis for understanding 'truth and beauty'. In this preliminary section, before we consider truth and beauty in the sonnets up to 126, we ask in what way sonnets 20 and 21 establish the basic logic of 'truth' and 'beauty' to ensure their natural alignment provides a necessary prerequisite for experiencing Shakespearean love.

After traversing the physical grounds of nature and the sexual dynamic of female and male with its requirement for increase, there followed the five sonnets 15 to 19 that reaffirm the natural precursors as basic if the Poet is to write deep and abiding love poetry. And we have seen that sonnet 17 specifically reiterates the dependence of 'beauty' as sensation and 'truth' as 'tongue' on 'some child of yours'.

The sonnet that follows immediately after the logical preconditions for writing is sonnet 20. We find that, like the conjoined sonnets 5 and 6 (connected by 'then') and 15 and 16 (connected by 'but'), sonnet 20 is a paired sonnet connected argumentatively by 'so' to sonnet 21.

But, of immediate significance, sonnet 20 introduces in its second line the male youth by his generic name, 'Master Mistress'[69]. The only other mention of the word mistress in the male sequence is in sonnet 126, where we met the 'sovereign mistress'. Is it a coincidence that Shakespeare parenthesises the discussion of truth and beauty in the male sequence by two sonnets carrying the word mistress?

A reading of the content of sonnet 20 confirms the logical order of priority established earlier. After the Poet calls nature the 'sovereign mistress' in sonnet 126 and the female the 'Mistress' in her sequence we now hear that the male is the 'Master Mistress'[70]. The implication of the name Master Mistress is that the male

---

[69] *In the 1609 edition, the two words 'Master Mistress' are capitalised and not hyphenated in contrast to their treatment in most modern editions:*
    A **woman's face with nature's own hand painted**,
    Hast thou the **Master Mistress** of my passion,
    A **woman's gentle heart** but not acquainted
    With shifting change as is **false women's fashion**, (*sonnet 20*, 1-4)

[70] *When in 'Twelfth Night' Orsino recognises Viola's superior cunning in adopting a male guise to correct his own psychological shortcomings, he calls her the 'Master's Mistress'. As in the sonnets, the name is an acknowledgment of the prior status Viola has over his tendency to be a fanciful male:*
    Orsino: Your **Master** quits you: and for your service done him,
    So much **against the mettle of your sex**,
    So far beneath your soft and tender **breeding**,
    And since you call'd me **Master**, for so long:
    Here is my hand, you shall from this time be
    Your **Master's Mistress**. (*Twelfth Night*, 5.1.2486-92)
    Viola's magisterial status is confirmed in the last words of the play when Orsino thanks Viola for maturing the 'fantastical...fancies' he was besotted by in the first lines of the first

has residual female characteristics consequent on his derivation from the female. The originary status of the female is borne out when the Poet states categorically that the male youth is 'created' in the first instance for a woman[71]. So the male's capacity to love is based in the female potentiality and from that foundation he experiences all other forms of love such as Platonic, homosexual, religious – depending on his innate disposition or learned inclination[72].

As we listen to the words of sonnet 20, we hear Shakespeare arguing that the name 'Master Mistress' identifies the youth as a male derived from the female in nature for the purposes of increase. Shakespeare's understanding conforms to the biological status of the female over the male. Again it seems Shakespeare, from his close observance of nature, appreciates the basic logic of human reproduction and persistence.

More significantly for what unfolds in the following sonnets and in his plays and poems, Shakespeare observes that the illogical inversion of the natural relationship of female to male in male-based myths typical of bible-fed religions such as the Hebrew, Christian and Muslim unwittingly reveals their genesis from within the human imagination[73].

Hence, as we seek to appreciate the impact of the injunction concerning

---

scene of the play:
> Orsino: **Cesario come**
> (For so you shall be while you are a man:)
> But when in other habits you are seen,
> Orsino's **Mistress**, and his **fancies Queen**. (*Twelfth Night*, 5.1.2555-8)

[71] *Sonnet 20 corrects the biblical order of Creation:*
And **for a woman wert thou first created**, (*sonnet 20, 9*)

[72] *Shakespeare's appreciation that the male derives from the female gives him an insight into both the female/male sexual dynamic and the feminine/masculine gender characteristics of human personality or personae. It is as if he intuits the fact that the female is the originary entity in the womb, where the fertilized egg needs hormonal intervention to form the male. The degree to which the egg is made male gives rise to the full spectrum from feminine males to masculine females. The consequence for any individual female or male is a predisposition to some combination of love based around increase and love based around gender relationships to form the complex of love possibilities of female/male, female/ female, male/male and personae-based love conditions, which are expressed as mind-based or religious emotions. Shakespeare examines many of the ramifications in his plays and poems.*

[73] *In 'Twelfth Night, or, What You Will' (to give the play its full title), Shakespeare deliberately focuses on the Epiphany or the moment when the infant Christ is celebrated as the man-God twelve days after his birth. 'Twelfth Night' has the identical twins Viola and Sebastian separated at sea (nature) and Viola cross-dressed as a male (God) to show the utility but ultimate conventionality of supplanting a male-God over nature. Viola's Godly correction of the love-struck Orsino out of a romantic infatuation with lachrymose Olivia into a maturity of mind is celebrated when she doffs her God-disguise and they make an inter-personal avowal of their 'marriage of true minds' at the play's end. They do not require the sanction of a Christian marriage – a fate reserved for the less philosophically robust Sebastian and Olivia a scene earlier.*

'truth and beauty' in sonnet 14, and its consequences for writing about love in sonnets 15 to 19, we are reminded in sonnet 20 of the originary status of the female. Shakespeare reaffirms in sonnet 20 his basic insight structured numerologically into the set of sonnets that the female is a unity whereas the male lacks unity until he acknowledges his logical relationship to the female. This is despite whatever other form of love the youth engages in through natural disposition or nurtured psychology.

With sonnet 20 reiterating the status of male to female, we turn to sonnet 21 to see what it has to say about truth and beauty. To appreciate the connection to truth in the first line of sonnet 21[74], we need to point out that there are two relevant words capitalised throughout the sonnet set. They are the 'Rose' (thirteen occurrences across both sequences) and the 'Muse' (seventeen occurrences confined to the male sequence). The 'Rose' enters the set in the first sonnet somewhat oxymoronically as 'beauty's Rose' as a metaphorical extension of the word beauty. 'Rose' also represents the sex organs and is an anagram of Eros, the Greek God of love, whose Roman counterpart Cupid appears in the final two sonnets 153 and 154.

The word 'Muse', significantly, occurs only in the Master Mistress sequence. Throughout, the Muse symbolizes poetry, verse, language, argument or any form of 'truth' as saying. And whereas the Rose appears in the second line of the set in the first sonnet (in keeping with the predominance of beauty throughout the increase sonnets), the Muse[75] is not introduced until the first line of sonnet 21 – after sonnets 15 to 19 introduce writing and sonnet 20 reiterates the priority of the female and the logic of increase.

In keeping with the basic themes of truth and beauty, we then find the word 'beauty' occurs in line 2 of sonnet 21. A brief look at the word 'beauty' in the second line reveals that the beauty addressed is 'a painted beauty'. This makes the 'beauty' in question not just an immediate effect of sensory input as in the Mistress sonnets but the deliberate enhancement of natural sensory information in the mind after negotiating layers of taste to arrive at the beauty of poetry or art. We will consider the implications of 'painted beauty' for the Poet's understanding of love in section 11.

So, two things are apparent from the combined use of the 'Muse' (for truth) and 'beauty' in sonnet 21. The first is that the Poet begins the treatment of truth in the Master Mistress sequence by talking of the potentiality of 'verse', a topic not addressed in the Mistress sequence. Additional to the dynamic of saying introduced in the Mistress sequence – as in verbalized swearing of oaths or even reasoning and thinking – in sonnets 20/21 the Poet begins to elaborate on the status of writing or verse that was introduced in sonnets 15 to 19.

When we look over the remainder of the Master Mistress sequence (sonnets

---

[74] *Sonnet 21 has 'Muse' in the first line and 'beauty' in the second line:*
    So is it not with me as with that **Muse**,
    Stirred by a painted **beauty** to his verse, (*sonnet 21*, 1-2)

[75] *In sonnet 38, the Poet distinguishes between his one Muse and the nine Muses of old. So we find the alien Poet's Muse (comprised of the nine Greek Muses) appears in sonnet 21, the Poet's Muse in sonnet 32 and so on where appropriate.*

22 to 126) we find the Poet mentions the words truth and beauty frequently as he develops his understanding of love. As we have seen, truth and beauty are structured so intentionally and so separately and with such purpose into the early and later parts of the female sequence, we need to ask how they are interrelated in the male sequence that deals with truth and beauty.

But, before we look more closely at truth and beauty in sections 10 and 11 respectively, it is worth commenting at this point in our investigation that we are focusing on 'truth' and 'beauty' in sonnets 20 to 126 rather than 'time', immortality or other conventional interpretative conceits. We can leave those concerns aside because the evident organization in Shakespeare's set of sonnets revealed so far indicates he understands that 'beauty' and 'truth' and consequently 'truth and beauty' represent the logical dynamic of the human mind.

To reiterate, we have the whole set configured as nature – called the 'sovereign mistress' – and the two sequences as 'Mistress' and 'Master Mistress', with the unequivocal increase argument ending at sonnet 14 with the words 'truth and beauty'. Then we have the mention of 'beauty' and 'truth' in sonnet 17 of the transitional increase-to-writing sonnets, and the division of the Mistress sonnets into those that mention 'beauty' and those that mention 'truth'.

On the basis of such seeming deliberateness on Shakespeare's part, we have revealed a trajectory from nature into the human mind that only prejudice could argue with. We appear more than validated in exploring the logical role of 'truth and beauty' in sonnets 20 to 126 – if we want to understand Shakespearean love.

The soundness of our findings so far lends direction to our exploration. As we consider the truth and beauty dynamic in sonnets 20 to 126 we can evaluate just how connected their content is to the preceding organisation in the set. And, as a double check, if an analysis of the Master Mistress sonnets in terms of truth and beauty reveals sensitivity to love commensurate with our intellectual and emotional response to the sonnets then we have achieved our goal of appreciating Shakespearean love.

We also hope to understand why the Poet devotes so many sonnets to the male youth (126 in all) compared to the female's 28. As we examine the lengthy Master Mistress sequence to 'truth and beauty' we might begin to understand the male's relationship to the female and why the love engendered by the male/masculine mind dynamic can be both beneficially idealistic and resolutely selfish. We might then appreciate why Shakespeare's plays depict the male/masculine dynamic as imaginatively inspirational but also responsible for the worst evils visited on humankind by humankind[76].

Sonnets 20/21 suggest Shakespeare purposely dedicates the majority of the male

---

[76] *There may be a connection between the 154 sonnets and the thirty-six plays in the 'Folio'. We have noted that the 1623 'Folio' contains fourteen comedies that successfully correct the iniquity in female and male relationships by applying Shakespeare's nature-based philosophy. In contrast, twenty-two plays (ten histories and twelve tragedies) focus on male-induced mayhem and murder. So it seems Shakespeare devotes more plays to male dissolution than to female resolution because problems with male-based excesses consequent on religion prove so intractable – both socially and politically.*

sequence from sonnets 20 to 126 to presenting the dynamic of truth and beauty in which language and the imagination are mind-based faculties. The realisation that language and art are mind-based activities whose manifestations are impermanent substitutes for natural processes establishes the basic criteria for representing Shakespearean love.

10 Teaching the Master Mistress about truth

If an understanding of incoming sensations (beauty) and the basic logic of language (truth) is imparted to the Poet by the female in her sequence to convert him from hate to love, what can we expect of love in the male sonnets that treat of 'truth and beauty'? If the female is a unity and the male is one less than unity what does the Poet do to rectify the male's self love criticised in the increase sonnets? In particular, how does the use of language in the male sonnets compare to the sworn/forsworn truth dynamic in the female sonnets?

Our expectation is that the Poet's appreciation of 'beauty' and 'truth' learnt from the Mistress will be taught to the male youth. It should be apparent from the first twenty sonnets to the Master Mistress that the Poet continually recycles his lessons for the benefit of the reluctant male youth – remember Venus' persistent but ultimately frustrated attempts to instruct Adonis in natural logic. Shakespeare's practice, when moving from one significant grouping of sonnets to the next, is to habitually reiterate lessons learnt in the previous group of sonnets and/or rehearse topics he will discuss in the succeeding sonnets.

Already in sonnet 14 we saw him anticipate the treatment of truth and beauty in the next group of sonnets and in sonnets 15 and 20 reiterate the increase argument. And it is in transitional sonnets such as 1, 14, 15/16, 19, 20/21, 126, 127, 137, 138, 152 and 154 that we might expect the reiterating/rehearsing to be most evident[77]. Shakespeare's canny patience as he teaches the natural logic of love to the Master Mistress gives his set of sonnets their wonderful combination of humanising intelligence and deeply realised emotions.

So, when considering sonnet 21, we should not be surprised Shakespeare's Poet begins by reasserting the dynamic of truth and beauty in its first two lines. And, as we look ahead to the instances of truth in the Master Mistress sequence, it is worth remembering that the first mention of truth at the end of sonnet 14 associates 'truth' with 'judgment' and 'knowledge' whereas it associates 'beauty' with 'art'.

When we scan from sonnet 20 to 126, we find there is a significant difference between the male and female sequences in the disposition of truth and beauty. In the male sequence, truth and beauty are intermixed throughout compared to the decidedly separate treatment they receive in the female sequence. So what has changed on the way from the female to the male sequence to explain the differing treatment of 'truth and beauty'?

We will first consider truth, and then in section 11 consider beauty.

On closer examination of the male sequence, we find the word 'truth' continues to refer to any form of language. Truth occurs more frequently in the male sequence than in the female sequence (17/6) as does beauty (57/9). And words like 'say' and 'says' occur in over twenty male sonnets (they appear in five female sonnets) and 'thought' and 'thoughts' in over twenty-five sonnets (compared to an appearance each of 'thought' and 'thoughts' in sonnet 147).

---

[77] *The interlacing of significant ideas at crucial points in the set and even the interweaving of sonnets from page to page in the 1609 edition is further evidence Shakespeare organised the set before publication in 1609 to present his substantive thoughts.*

The first sonnet to examine 'truth' after sonnet 21's reference to the Muse is sonnet 37. It mentions both 'truth' and 'beauty' in that order. It reiterates the basis for the youth's 'worth' in 'store' – or the increase dynamic – by recounting a father's delight in his child's 'worth and truth'. It states that whatever – if any – of the combination of 'beauty (sensory effects), birth (station in life), or wealth (material means), or wit (truth as language)' the youth has as his inherited dispositions, his father affirms that his 'love' is 'engrafted to this store'[78]. For the youth to make his 'father' (metaphorically the Poet) 'ten times happy' he needs to accept the natural basis for his burgeoning 'glory' – including his potential to mature in love.

Sonnet 41 is the next to mention 'truth' and, in keeping with Shakespeare's focus on truth and beauty, it includes 'beauty'. Sonnets 41 and 42 perform the obverse role in the Master Mistress sequence to sonnets 133/134 and 143/144 in the Mistress sequence. They remind the youth of his logical relationship to the female since his ability to understand and love is based on the natural relationship of beauty and truth generated in her sequence.

We find that sonnet 41 deals with the relationship of female and male as persons with the question as to whether the male responds appropriately or inappropriately to a woman saying no[79]. Then sonnet 42 complements the relationship of persons in sonnet 41 with the relationship between feminine and masculine personae of the mind where the 'joy' is that all can be 'one' in the Poet's mature love[80]. We can

---

[78] *Sonnet 37 is typical of Shakespeare's sonnets that both look back and look forward as they make their argument to the idealistic youth. In the interrelationship of ideas, Shakespeare mimics the generational dynamic where the son has some of his fathers characteristics and some new:*

> As a decrepit **father** takes delight,
> To see his active **child** do deeds of youth,
> So I, made lame by Fortune's dearest spite
> Take all my comfort of thy **worth and truth**.
> For whether **beauty, birth, or wealth, or wit**,
> Or any of these all, or all, or more
> Intitled in their parts, do crowned sit,
> **I make my love engrafted to this store:** (*sonnet 37*, 1-8)

Sonnet 37 is followed by sonnet 38 that adds to the 'nine Muses of old' one more Muse, which is the Poet's Muse derived from the Mistress sequence: $9+1 = 10 = 1+0 = 1$:

> Be thou the **tenth Muse, ten times more in worth**
> **Than those old nine** which rhymers invoke, (*sonnet 38*, 9,10)

[79] *Sonnet 41 describes the attraction between a female and male when the male abuses his beauty against her refusal. The 'woes' in line 7 is critical to the meaning of the sonnet – some editors emend 'woes' to 'woos' and 'he' to 'she' in line 8 completely undermining Shakespeare's critique of male-based excesses:*

> Gentle thou art, and therefore to be won,
> Beauteous thou art, therefore to be assailed.
> And **when a woman woes, what woman's son,**
> **Will sourly leave her till he have prevailed.** (*sonnet 41*, 5-8)

[80] *In sonnet 42, Shakespeare mocks the tendency to dissociate personae by idealising them as distinct entities:*

> If I lose thee, my loss is my love's gain,

recall the same pattern of persons and then personae in sonnets 133/134 and in sonnets 143/144.

Sonnet 41 talks first of the youth abusing his 'beauteous' appearance willfully for temptation and assault. The male youth's intentional exploitation of 'beauty' for selfish ends shifts the Poet's analysis of 'beauty' as 'fair' and 'foul' in the Mistress' sequence to new levels of sensory manipulation. If the Mistress in her sequence was called either fair or foul because of mind-based prejudice, the male youth now callously acts out that prejudice.

The crunch comes toward the end of sonnet 41 when the Poet itemises the breaking of 'a two fold truth'[81]. Firstly, the youth abuses his 'beauty' to tempt the Mistress until he prevails over her and, secondly, by using his 'beauty' in that deceitful manner the youth proves false to the Poet's nature-based hopes for love founded in rational behaviour. Here, 'truth' is the interrelationship of susceptibility and deception exploited by the youth. The idealistic misconstruing of female/male biology can only be resolved by recovering the natural dynamic for love laid out in the overall structure of the set and in the first nineteen sonnets.

When we move to the next sonnet that mentions 'truth', sonnet 48, we find it deflates the idealistic dream of truth as a singular 'prize'. The aged Poet recounts, somewhat tongue-in-cheek, that he 'thrust' each 'trifle', or every bit of contrary evidence, under 'truest bars' to conceal from 'falsehood' – or the possibility of being proven false – that the ideal is inevitably 'thievish'.

Yet, as sonnet 48 continues, even if the Poet has matured his own idealism, he realises he cannot always restrain the idealism of the Master Mistress from causing the 'greatest grief'. Even though adolescent idealism is the 'best of dearest' (or most costly as sonnet 31 explains) its headstrong headiness proves difficult to curtail.

The irony sonnet 48 plays with is that to unnecessarily restrain the youth would be to deny the Poet once had adolescent expectations that are now memories 'within the gentle closure of my breast'. The youthful wish that 'truth' be a singular 'prize', and not the dynamic of saying that argues true and false, 'proves thievish' of the idealised love the youth holds so 'dear'. Even though such love can prove very costly in practice, the youth needs to experience it for himself to mature his understanding and emotions.

> And losing her, my friend hath found that loss,
> Both find each other, and I lose both twain,
> And both for my sake lay on me this cross,
>   But **here's the joy, my friend and I are one**,
>   Sweet flattery, then **she loves but me alone**. (*sonnet 42*, 9-14)

---

[81] *Sonnet 41 concludes with a graphic example of how the senses (beauty) form ideas (a two-fold truth) in the mind. Shakespeare shows that the interrelationship of sensory effects and ideas is based directly on the female/male dynamic in nature:*

> Aye me, but yet thou mightst my seat forbear,
> And chide **thy beauty, and thy straying youth**,
> Who lead thee in their riot even there
> Where **thou art forced to break a two-fold truth**:
>   Hers by **thy beauty tempting** her to thee,
>   Thine by **thy beauty being false** to me. (*sonnet 41*, 9-14)

'Truth' reoccurs with 'beauty' again in the second line of sonnet 54. Then, in its last line, 'truth' re-emerges as a process of distillation after the Poet presents contrasting sensations to the youth's quirky mind. In the previous thirteen lines beauty and its symbol the Rose intertwine to reveal the slippage between 'sweet Roses' and 'Canker blooms' that present sensations or 'odours' to the mind to incite conflicting thoughts. Sweet Roses perpetuate themselves through increase whereas Canker blooms 'die to themselves'.

If the youth remains a 'Canker bloom' he has the secondary consolation that, when aged, a record of his beauty may still be available in the 'truth' or conflicted thoughts distilled 'by' the Poet's 'verse'[82]. The allusion in the second line to the beauty of verse and art as 'sweet ornament' sublimated from the dynamic of 'truth' is only 'sweet' if the youth appreciates the allegory of the two Roses.

Sonnet 60 confirms that we are dealing with 'nature's truth'. The Poet states that 'beauty's brow' loses its youth and dies in 'time' leaving the Poet's verse as a written record of the youth's youthful 'worth'. 'Nature's truth' implies the female and male dynamic – which results in increase – establishes the logic of true and false in the human mind that enables the Poet to write verse to 'praise' the youth as youth. But, as we saw in sonnet 138, the reliability of the Poet's word is no substitute for increase, so truth is only as rigorous as the youth's confidence in nature. As sonnet 138 explains, the Poet understands that lying-with develops a lying wit[83].

Sonnet 62 also has both 'truth' and 'beauty'. The Poet recalls 'mine own' possessive 'sin of self love' when he was a youth. He describes not only his memory of iniquitous 'self love', he acknowledges that the youth reminds him of the 'beauty' of those 'days'. He struggles with the temptation of 'painting my age' to hide his 'tanned antiquity'.

But in sonnet 62 the Poet's intent is to both sympathise with the recalcitrance that is youth and provide him with a salutary lesson to rectify the 'sin' of male-based immaturity. The delusion generated in the Poet's mind of eternal youth and self 'worth', where youth 'thinks no face so gracious is as mine', makes 'no truth of such account' or voids accountability.

The confusion of truth with beauty is the utmost 'sin' because the singular

---

[82] *Sonnet 54 begins by describing how 'beauty' or incoming sensations when subjected to the dynamic of 'truth' can become 'beauteous' or the mind-based sensations of 'verse' the Poet calls 'sweet ornament':*

Oh how much more doth **beauty** beauteous seem,
By that sweet ornament which **truth** doth give, (*sonnet 54, 1-2*)
The couplet confirms that when the youth's physical beauty fades, it is through the Poet's 'verse' that his beauty is made into a 'sweet ornament' so that the 'truth' dynamic between 'sweet' and 'canker' can be distilled or understood:
And so of you, **beauteous** and lovely youth,
When that shall vade, **by verse distils your truth**. (*sonnet 54, 13-14*)

[83] *The apparent typo in the last line of sonnet 23, where 'wit' and 'with', which seem transposed by the 1609 compositors, begs the question as to whether Shakespeare wittily associated 'wit' with the mind's 'eyes' and 'with' with 'loves':*
O learn to read what silent love hath writ,
To hear **with** eyes belongs to love's fine **wit**. (*sonnet 23, 13-14*)

beauty of youth becomes equated with 'truth' and the give and take of accounting that is truth or saying is short-circuited. Here, in this ledger of accusations against the sin of idealised 'self love', Shakespeare points the finger at the mono-male God (mentioned four sonnets back in 58 as a slave-maker) who takes truth unto himself, thus hereticising counter-argument.

Sonnet 66 is the most determined truth sonnet in the Master Mistress sequence. It clarifies the confusion surrounding truth especially when the natural logic of argument is ignored and truth is rendered singular. It gives a three-quatrain list of opposed ideas the Poet says are typical of language as truth. In a sonnet of unique form, where a litany of 'and's emphasises the logic of truth, the Poet cites eleven instances of oppositions typical of propositional language. He specifically includes the tendency to misrepresent 'simple-Truth' as 'Simplicity' and reiterates the lesson from the Mistress sequence that even the 'purest faith' is inevitably 'forsworn'[84].

'Simple-Truth' is the everyday determination of true and false through language. The Poet insists truth as saying should not be confused with 'Simplicity' or overly idealistic attempts to associate 'truth' with the singular sensations or emotions generated within the mind, which are a form of beauty. The Poet's responsibility is to convince the youth through argument of the direct relation between youth's simplistic take on truth and his selfish desire to be 'alone'[85].

---

[84] *In sonnet 66, Shakespeare breaks completely with usual sonnet forms to illustrate the 'endless jar' between right and wrong that Ulysses says is 'Justice' in 'Troilus and Cressida':*
> Tir'd with all these for restful death I cry,
> As to behold desert a beggar born,
> And needy Nothing trimmed in jollity,
> **And purest faith unhappily forsworn,**
> And gilded honor shamefully misplaced,
> And maiden virtue rudely strumpeted,
> And right perfection wrongfully disgraced,
> And strength by limping sway disabled,
> And art made tongue-tied by authority,
> And Folly (Doctor-like) controlling skill,
> **And simple-Truth miscalled Simplicity,**
> And captive-good attending Captain ill.
>> Tir'd with all these, from these would I be gone,
>> Save that to die, I leave my love alone. (*sonnet 66*)

[85] *Shakespeare's use of the word 'alone' meaning 'on one's own' recurs in sonnet 84 and in 'Love's Labour's Lost'. Editors remove the comma after 'alone' in sonnet 84 to make it sound as if the youth is unique:*
> Who is it that says most, which can say more,
> Than this rich praise, that **you alone, are you,**
> In whose confine immured is the **store,**
> Which **should example where your equal grew,** (*sonnet 84*, 1-4)

The editors of modern editions of 'Love's Labour's Lost' reveal their misunderstanding of Shakespeare's philosophy when they amend 'alone, alone' to the meaningless exclamation 'allons, allons':
> Berowne: **Alone, Alone** sowed Cockle, reaped no Corn,

The Poet mocks the youth by pretending he is 'tired' of arguing with him, and would rather die than persist in such frustrating verbal interplay or 'truth'. But then the Poet would fall foul of his own injunction about increase and hence 'love'. The Poet's 'death' would 'leave' the youth 'alone' to face the consequences of being 'alone' without the opportunity to appreciate the logic of increase that drives the oppositional dynamic of language or 'truth'.

Up until now, Shakespeare's Poet has explained what he means by 'truth' and why his understanding of truth is consistent with human nature based in nature. Although he heralds 'painted beauty' in sonnet 21, in keeping with Shakespeare's exemplary patience in the sonnets that mention 'truth', he continues to convey to the Master Mistress what he has learnt from the Mistress about sensory beauty and the logic of truth. He wants the youth to grasp fully the implications of confusing beauty as sensations with truth as saying.

In the next 'truth' sonnet 69, the Poet relates truth to beauty as poetry or art. He picks up on the suggestion in sonnet 54 that the 'sweet ornament' of beauty is available in the Poet's verse. Shakespeare knows he is using the dynamic of 'truth' or saying to point to the form of beauty that was associated with poetry and art in sonnets 14 and 21. This is the beauty generated in the human mind and expressed in words or paint or music.

So in sonnet 69, the Poet begins by drawing attention to the youth's 'outward' parts that 'the world's eye doth view', or his sensory beauty, and accepts that outwardly they 'want nothing'. The Poet concedes that neither the 'thought of hearts' nor the 'voice of souls' can 'mend' the youth's appearance as it utters a 'bare truth' or simplistic effect that even 'foes' can admire.

But, as we move down sonnet 69, we hear the Poet claim that giving so much value to the 'bare truth' of appearance creates a problem. What is taken for 'truth' by the romantic 'heart' or idealizing 'soul' is simplistic, and the simplistic view of truth was dismissed in sonnet 66. If those 'tongues' look further into the mind of the youth than 'the eye has shown', their 'outward praise' will be confounded by the inward confusion that is the youth's mind.

As we continue down sonnet 69 we hear Poet insist on the use of 'truth' as the process of saying that this is or this is not (as we saw in sonnet 137). If 'they look into the beauty of thy mind' or the effects that show in the youth's 'deeds' as poetry or art, their 'thoughts' would be 'churled' (sic) or soured by the youth's niggard husbandry of his 'soil' or earthboundness. To the youth's 'fair flowers' or appearance they would have to 'add the rank smell of weeds' emanating from his denatured idealising mind[86].

And Justice always whirls in equal measure:
Light Wenches may prove plagues to men forsworn,
  If so, our Copper buys no better treasure. (*Love's Labour's Lost*, 4.3.1734-7)
  The word 'alone' characterises the condition of being alone, or sundered from the natural logic of increase in nature. In a colourful version of the increase argument, Berowne advises that 'men', if they sow their cocks 'alone', will reap 'no corn' from women's 'treasure'.

[86] *Sonnet 69 inter-relates outward appearance (beauty), plus truth in action where 'tongues' confound 'praise' and 'beauty' that is in the 'mind'. Shakespeare could not be more*

The youth's 'odour' does not match his 'show' because the bottom line is that he 'dost common grow' or is based in nature through increase. Only when the youth understands how the logic of beauty derives from nature and the sexual dynamic to form poetry and art in the mind will the disjunction between his beautiful appearance and his 'deeds' be rectified.

Sonnet 72, which mentions only 'truth', reasserts the conditional nature of verse. The Poet asks that the youth forget him and his works because in themselves they mean nothing. Only in the context of his natural logic does his love have meaning and that is the 'niggard truth'. In keeping with the logic of truth, if the youth devises 'some virtuous lie' then that would be truer to the Poet's worth than the overwrought worth the youth and others place on the 'word'.

The dynamic of truth, which Ulysses calls the 'jar' between true and false, is on full display in sonnet 96. It lays out the logic of saying where 'some say thy fault is youth' and 'some say thy grace is youth'[87]. The youth's idealistic errors of judgment are 'translated' to simplistic 'truths' and taken for 'true things'. He would not be the first idealistic youth to lead 'gazers' away by disguising his wolfish corruption of truth as a 'Lamb' – with Shakespeare's obvious reference to the biblical Christ. Again the Poet acknowledges that the youth's error is one the Poet made himself when adolescent, so his argument is full of sympathy for the untutored mind.

---

specific about the logic of beauty/truth/beauty, which is founded on the sexual dynamic in nature – as the last line affirms:

> **Their outward thus with outward praise is crowned,**
> But those same **tongues** that give thee so thine own,
> In other accents do this **praise confound**
> **By seeing farther than the eye hath shown.**
> **They look into the beauty of thy mind,**
> And that in guess they measure by thy **deeds,**
> Then churls their thoughts (although their eyes were kind)
> To thy **fair flower** add the **rank smell of weeds,**
>> But why thy odour matcheth not thy show,
>> **The soil is this, that thou dost common grow.** (*sonnet 69*, 5-14)

[87] *Shakespeare's appreciation of the oppositional logic of truth in the first four lines of sonnet 96 sets up the critique of religion in the remainder of the sonnet:*

> Some **say** thy **fault** is youth, some wantonness,
> Some **say** thy **grace** is youth and gentle sport,
> Both **grace and faults** are loved of more and less:
> Thou mak'st **faults graces**, that to thee resort: (*sonnet 96*, 1-4)

The same error occurs in sonnet 96 as in sonnet 66 – mistaking 'truth' for simplicity – with Shakespeare noting that the same simplifications are evident in biblical dogma:

> So are those **errors** that in thee are seen,
> **To truths translated, and for true things deemed.**
> How many **Lambs** might the stern **Wolf** betray,
> If like a **Lamb** he could his looks translate.
> **How many gazers mightst thou lead away,**
> If thou wouldst use the strength of all thy state?
>> But do not so, I love thee in such sort,
>> As **thou being mine, mine is thy good report**. (*sonnet 96*, 7-14)

Then, sonnet 101 emphasises the relevance for love of the lessons the Poet gives the Master Mistress in truth and beauty in the preceding sonnets[88]. And we can see that sonnet 101 differentiates specifically between 'truth' as a process of discrimination through writing ('pencil') and 'beauty' as an artistic effect based on 'colour'. It criticises those who 'kill' truth by dissociating it from language when they confuse truth with 'beauty' or imaginary ideals in the mind.

Better than that, in sonnet 101 the Poet definitively associates the correct appreciation of truth and beauty with the nature-based 'love' he argues for and expresses in his sonnets. He insists that his 'love depends' on the correct understanding of 'truth and beauty'. At this stage in the sequence we have reached the inner workings of the mind where the deepest love flourishes freely so long as the natural workings of the mind at full pitch are understood and sustained.

Sonnet 110 confirms the benefits of experiencing love in a natural light. If the Poet has 'looked on truth / Askance and strangely', it has enabled him to experience 'love' at a depth and greater consistency than that wrongly attributed to the male God. But now, instead of being a 'slave' to a tyrant male God (as recounted in sonnet 58) his experience is the natural equivalent to a 'God in love'. No wonder Shakespeare's reader's feel for the depth of love expressed in the sonnets yet cannot understand its genesis and development from the overwrought emotions of youthful idealism to its mature experience and expression under the tutelage of the Mistress and then the Poet.

We have noted the marked difference between the Poet's attitude to the Mistress compared to his treatment of the Master Mistress when talking of 'truth'. The Mistress teaches the Poet the logic of truth. In her sequence we saw that the act of swearing characterises the truth dynamic in establishing the difference between true and false because even a sworn oath might later be forsworn.

Swearing, though, is not the focus of the Master Mistress sequence. 'Swear', 'swears' or 'swearing' are not mentioned in the male sonnets although 'forsworn' appears in sonnets 66 and 88, and 'vow' and 'vows' in sonnet 89, 115 and 123 – far fewer times proportionately than in the Mistress sequence.

Instead 'argument', a word not mentioned in the female sonnets, occurs six times (sonnets 38, 76, 79, 100, 103, 105) with the Poet arguing continually with the male youth throughout the sequence. This is in keeping with the attitude of instruction adopted by the Poet toward the intractable male. The use of truth as argument is evident in the number of logical connectives between pairs or groups of sonnets and the extended arguments of the increase group (1 to 14), the increase

---

[88] *Sonnet 101 presents the clearest expression of the distinct roles of truth and beauty in the sonnets to the male:*

Oh truant **Muse** what shall be thy amends,
For **thy neglect of truth in beauty died?**
Both **truth and beauty on my love depends:**
So dost thou too, and therein dignified:
Make answer Muse, wilt thou not haply say
Truth needs no colour with his colour fixed,
Beauty no pencil, beauty's truth to lay:
But best is best, if never intermixed. (*sonnet 101*, 1-8)

and poetry group (15 to 19) and the alien Poet group (78 to 86).

We have seen that references to 'time' occur only in the male sequence as does the only reference to the male God of biblical religions. The Muse also occurs only in the male sequence in association with verse and argument, and the discussion about verse is confined to the male sequence. Significantly, immortality of the 'soul' is addressed only in the male sequence.

The common ground amongst these secondary concerns is that they all function as mind-based conventions established through the logic of language or the dynamic of 'swearing' and so are capable of being disestablished through argument that leads to forswearing. For instance, natural time intervals such as the day, month and year are rendered calculable as minutes, hours and weeks – as Shakespeare acknowledges in sonnet 12 ('the clock that tells the time') and sonnet 60 ('so do our minutes hasten to their end').

To the functional conventions that allow us to measure time accurately, we can add those that invert the natural order. The first three commandments of Mosaic Law conventionalise the usurpation of natural female priority by the male God to embed dictatorial power. Closely related is the belief in the immortality of the soul that conventionalises the logic of increase for the management of the overly psychological mind.

All conventions established through language are cemented in place by the written word. Hence the nine Greek Muses compartmentalise creative capacities. But, as Shakespeare knows well, books as objects of veneration are not much more than 'black lines' on the page (sonnet 63). So, Shakespeare adds his tenth Muse (in sonnet 38) because she, as the only female Muse answerable to nature, reasserts the natural relationship of precursor female to male.

When T. S. Eliot accuses Shakespeare of having a 'rag-bag philosophy' and no system of morals, because Eliot prefers the 'serious philosophy' of Dante's conventionalised Christian morality apparent in the very hierarchical *Divine Comedy*, we can begin to appreciate why Eliot gets it so wrong about Shakespeare[89]. Eliot buys into the mind-based male God convention-bound morality supported by self-serving commandments, which sonnet 21 warns against. But the deeply bedded misogyny behind those commandments makes them murderous as norms for personal, social and political justice – as Shakespeare demonstrates in his histories and tragedies[90].

Little wonder Eliot cannot see why Shakespeare refuses to accept the purely mind-based mores of biblical morality but prefers the unarguable givens of nature and the dynamic of female and male he lays out in his sonnets and makes the basis of his poems and plays. Shakespeare recognised in the religious mayhem of the Reformation all about him that the short-term advantage of such beliefs is far outweighed by the long-term evil visited on nature and natural values – especially

[89] T. S. Eliot, Introduction, G. Wilson Knight, *The Wheel of Fire*, London, Methuen, 1965.

[90] *This is also the syndrome the American Constitution was designed to prevent as is the ring-fencing of Anglicism and Catholicism in Buckingham Palace and Vatican City respectively.*

women's rights and the opportunity to achieve mature love. Instead, Shakespeare's logical understanding of 'truth' provides the natural basis for morality in a global society.

So we can begin to appreciate why Shakespeare structures his two sequences around the dynamic of beauty and truth and then truth and beauty after establishing the givens of nature, the female/male dynamic and increase. Love can only be free when the Poet establishes a basis for truth and beauty founded in the natural circumstances in which humankind resides.

Having followed Shakespeare as he explains the logic of truth to the Master Mistress and accounts for the rest of the concepts such as time and God that appear there, we can now listen as he demonstrates the logic of beauty for the benefit of male youth – or the masculine aspect of the human mind – female or male. We will watch as Shakespeare uses his deep understanding of the art of poetry and drama to give rigorous but exquisite expression to his nature-based experience and understanding of love.

Shakespeare combines the treatment of truth as argument and beauty as art in the sonnets from 20 to 126. We have examined first his analysis of truth as an argumentative process for bringing rigour and vigour to Shakespearean love.

11 What the Master Mistress has to learn about beauty and love

Shakespeare's sonnets do not convey their deeply affective emotions solely by reminding us that we increase, require sensory input and use language to swear oaths and argue a case. What form of mind-based sensations and what type of love, then, are associated with the male in his sequence that might allow the Poet and Master Mistress – and Mistress – to arrive at a marriage of true minds?

We have observed the Poet as he learns the truth dynamic of swearing and forswearing from the Mistress in her sequence and then applies it in the Master Mistress sequence to argue for his nature-based philosophy. So, what happens to the singularity of incoming sensations the Poet calls 'beauty' in the female sonnets from 127 to 137 when we move to the male sonnets from 20 to 126?

If we examine the instances of the word 'beauty' in sonnets 20 to 126 around one-third continue to refer to the appearance of the youth and the other two-thirds refer to the form of beauty identified as 'art' in sonnet 14 and 'painted beauty' in sonnet 21. There are references in the Mistress truth sonnets to 'Art' in sonnet 139 and 'painting' in sonnet 146, but as yet they are not identified with the form of 'beauty' that is generated in the mind. The two references presume on the Poet's examination of beauty as 'art' in sonnets 20 to 126. Again we see the significance of sonnets 15 to 19 for accommodating these seemingly presumptuous uses of language.

We have already commented on Shakespeare's practice of anticipating and revisiting topics such as 'nature', 'increase', and 'truth and beauty'. In his treatment of increase, for instance, he places the increase argument right at the beginning of the set because increase is implied in the sexual division of male from female in nature. Increase is then made a precondition for writing in sonnets 15 to 19 and then its significance is reaffirmed a number of times in sonnets 20 to 126 and alluded to a few times in sonnets 127 to 152.

Likewise, when we follow the trajectory of sensory beauty throughout the 154 sonnets we find Shakespeare using the same investigative and instructive method. His Poet explains how he learnt the dynamic of sensory beauty in the Mistress sonnets and the Poet then uses the appeal of sensory beauty as leverage on the male youth in the increase sonnets. We will now see the Poet using sensory beauty as a point of comparison in the Master Mistress sonnets that deal with truth and beauty as he argues for the significance of the nature-based role of 'beauty' as poetry or art.

So, whereas the Poet uses beauty in the increase sonnets to appeal to the youth's pride in his own appearance, in the sonnets that teach the youth 'truth and beauty' he warns the youth not to be beguiled by outright flattery. In the alien Poet sonnets 78 to 86, particularly, the 'other' writer's blatant flattery of the youth's appearance is contrasted to the Poet's examination of the qualities of the youth's mind[91]. We have seen how the Poet critiques the youth's understanding of 'truth'

---

[91] *Sonnet 79 specifically examines the instances where the other Poet merely re-invents the youth's beauty. In effect the other Poet steals what he writes about in praise directly from the youth, whereas the Poet appreciates that a much deeper understanding of human nature is needed to create insightful and emotive verse:*

and now we will see how he challenges the youth's appreciation of art and poetry or the sensations in the mind the Poet also calls 'beauty'.

As we consider the sonnets that examine the relationship between truth and beauty generated in the mind, we will need to explain Shakespeare's use of the same word 'beauty' for two activities in the human mind that are similar but distinct. Just what is the additional function of 'beauty', which in the Mistress sequence means externally generated sensory effects, as the Poet extends its use to refer to sensations such as intuitions and emotions evoked in the mind by ideas that develop in the mind.

We will consider Shakespeare's determination that because incoming sensations and enminded sensations are both singular aesthetic effects unmediated by thought, they have the same unbidden repercussion within the mind, so he calls both of them 'beauty'. From what we have already gleaned about truth, combining the two forms of sensation under the one word 'beauty' is more exact than miscalling beauty truth.

If we look first at sonnet 24, we will see just how much the concept of beauty has developed from representing incoming sensations in the Mistress sequence to symbolising sensations in the mind induced by the Poet's reflections on the youth's beauty in the Master Mistress sequence. No other sonnet in the male sequence focuses so resolutely on beauty in the mind.

The Poet claims the youth's 'form' is inscribed on the 'table of my heart'[92]. And from the first line where the Poet says 'mine eye' has 'played the painter', we can see that the whole sonnet describes imaginative effects within the mind. Sonnet 24 prepares us for all the following evocations of artistic practice down the Master

> **Yet what of thee thy Poet doth invent,**
> **He robs thee of, and pays it thee again,**
> He lends thee virtue, and he stole that word,
> From thy behaviour, beauty doth he give
> And found it in thy cheek: he can afford
> No praise to thee, but what in thee doth live.
> **Then thank him not for that which he doth say,**
> **Since what he owes thee, thou thy self dost pay.** (*sonnet 79*, 7-14)

[92] *Sonnet 24 is a picture gallery of artistic effects on display within the Poet's mind:*
> **Mine eye** hath **played the painter** and hath **steeld,**
> **Thy beauty's form in table of my heart,**
> My body is the **frame** wherein 'tis held,
> And **perspective it is best Painter's art.**
> For through the **Painter** must you see his skill,
> To find where your true **Image pictur'd lies,**
> Which in my bosom's shop is **hanging still,**
> That hath his **windows glazed** with thine eyes:
> Now see what good-turns eyes for eies have done,
> **Mine eyes have drawn thy shape,** and thine for me
> Are **windows to my breast,** where-through the Sun
> Delights to peep, to gaze therein on thee.
> **Yet eyes this cunning want to grace their art**
> **They draw but what they see, know not the heart.** (*sonnet 24*)

Mistress sonnets that are metaphors for the 'beauty' or aesthetic effects occurring in the human mind. By describing the mind-based effects so vividly in artistic terms in sonnet 24, it is as if they are clamouring to be expressed in poetry on the page or in an artwork.

We can note that the word 'cunning' in the couplet of sonnet 24 reminds us that Shakespeare interconnects the eyes of the mind – both sensory and imaginative – with the sexual eye of either sex. The trajectory from nature and the sexual dynamic of female and male energises the minds of the Poet and his youth. The passage from the external world of the sensory eye into the mind and into the heart, and then into what sonnet 27 calls the 'soul's imaginary sight', completes the circle as the imagining soul and sexual instinct cohabit and radiate from within the body. Sonnet 24 pictures for the Master Mistress the easy inter-penetrability of body and mind that distinguishes Shakespeare's comprehensive nature-based love from simplistic body-based hedonistic love or mind-based Platonic love.

Returning to the exploration of beauty, we find, when scanning the Master Mistress sequence, that the mind-based extension to the meaning of 'beauty' beyond everyday sensory input is cast in a number of differing ways to reflect the full palette of imaginative effects. So in sonnet 24 we hear of beauty in terms of 'perspective', 'painter's art' and 'image pictured'.

Then in sonnet 53 we are told that 'on Helen's cheek all art of beauty set'. This is followed in sonnet 54 by 'that sweet ornament which truth doth give'. As we have seen in the truth analysis of the Master Mistress sonnets, the image of the youth as ornament is a consequence of the truth dynamic of true and false being resolved into singular or artistic effects in the mind.

When we turn to sonnet 62, we find it associates beauty specifically with art when it says 'painting my age with beauty of thy days'[93]. Then sonnet 63 associates beauty with poetic effects when it says 'his beauty in these black lines be seen'.

The Poet brings 'love' directly into the potentiality of poetry in sonnet 65 when he follows its references to painting and writing by talking of 'beauty' where 'in black ink my love may still shine bright'[94]. Sonnet 67 goes further when it characterises as 'false painting' the negative effects of mind-based sensations. It is seconded by sonnet 68's dismissal of the 'false Art' of male-based ideals in favour of nature-based 'beauty'.

---

[93] *Sonnet 62 shows Shakespeare revisiting the 'self love' syndrome afflicting the youth in the increase sonnets:*

> But when **my glass shows me my self** indeed
> Beated and chopped with tanned antiquity,
> **Mine own self love** quite contrary I read
> **Self, so self loving were iniquity,**
>   **'Tis thee (my self) that for my self I praise,**
>   **Painting my age with beauty of thy days.** (*sonnet 62, 9-14*)

[94] *Sonnet 65 considers the irony or natural 'miracle' that the Poet's love will survive all forms of artifice because his understanding of 'beauty' is anchored in the natural dynamic he lays down in the 'black ink' of his sonnets:*

> O none, unless this miracle have might,
> That **in black ink my love may still shine bright.** (*sonnet 65, 13-14*)

Sonnet 77 reiterates the relationship of this mind-based form of 'beauty' to poetry with its 'commit to these waste blacks' because, like 'children nursed', ideas can be 'delivered from thy brain' onto the pages of a 'book'. A couple of sonnets away within the alien Poet group, sonnet 79 laments the robbery that is false art as the Poet accuses the other Poet of merely mimicking the physical appearance of the youth – 'from thy behaviour, beauty doth he give' – rather than evoking the depths of the youth's 'gentle grace'.

Still within the nine alien Poet sonnets, sonnet 83 emphasises the relationship between 'speaking' and 'silence' – or saying and not-saying. Although the other writer's 'modern quill' sells the youth 'short', the youth fails to understand that the Poet remains 'mute' so as not to 'impair' the beauty of body and mind that constitutes the youth's 'life'. Again, the Poet rejects the false 'painting' ('painting' is mentioned twice in the first two lines) that mimics the appearance of the ideal young man in favour of the 'worth' that in you 'doth grow'. The natural extension of the youth's appearance through increase into the emotive operations of the mind is the only way to generate deeply felt beauty, and hence love, that is beyond compare[95].

Then sonnet 106 again makes a connection not seen in the Mistress sequence when it relates 'beauty' to 'making beautiful old rhyme'. To add to the emphasis on beauty as poetry or art, sonnet 115 goes further with its dismissive 'tan sacred beauty'. The Poet discounts imaginary religious love by reminding us of the 'millioned accidents' of increase that 'creep in twixt vows'. Ultimately increase, as sonnet 14 predicts, shows up 'false art' (sonnets 67/68) and hence the mind-based customs welded together by overly idealised 'vows'.

And there are other sonnets that do not specifically mention beauty but refer to sensations that either make themselves apparent only in the mind or when transposed into poetry or art. So, in sonnet 31 we see the word 'images', in sonnet 47 'thy picture', in sonnet 59 'your image in some antique book', and in sonnet 61 'thy image'. Sonnet 78 emphasises the importance of inner sensations for all humankind when the Poet says the male youth is 'all my art'.

In sonnet 82 of the alien Poet group, the Poet even talks of 'gross painting' and associates it with the 'strained…Rhetoric' in the 'dedicated words which writers use'. As we draw near the end of the male sequence, in sonnet 125 we hear the Poet say he 'knows no art but mutual render' that comes from an uncompromised love – 'only me for thee'. He contrasts his natural expression of love with the pomp

---

[95] *Sonnet 83 at the heart of the alien Poet group compares the 'painting' other Poets produce from the beauty of the youth to the unspoken beauty the Poet evokes – even if he remains effectively mute so as to avoid the 'tomb' of an idealised death:*

This silence for my sin you did impute,
What shall be most my glory being dumb,
For I impair not beauty being mute,
When others would give life, and bring a tomb.
There **lives more life in one of your fair eyes,**
Than both your Poets can in praise devise. (*sonnet 83,* 9-14)

and architecture built by those preening themselves for 'eternity'[96]. Again the Poet rejects the 'form and favour' propping up a supposed 'true soul'. Instead he argues for the direct line of descent without 'seconds' from nature into the depths of the human mind.

So, Shakespeare lists a variety of singular artistic and poetic effects under the name of 'beauty' in the Master Mistress sequence. The number of differing mind-based effects contrasts quite markedly with the more specific focus on the five senses in the Mistress sequence. Although the Poet reiterates his findings about sensory 'beauty' for the purpose of instruction in the Master Mistress sequence, there is now a significant emphasis on beauty as poetry and art.

We have noted Shakespeare's method of reiteration and rehearsal as the Poet instructs the reluctant male youth. The intermixing of old lessons with new lessons is a reflection of the difficulty the youth (or anyone) has in understanding the illusively simple love trajectory Shakespeare observes from nature through the sexual dynamic and increase to beauty and truth and then truth and beauty mediated through the artifacts of writing or deeply conceptual painting.

Shakespeare seems to accept that the most difficult aspect of his philosophy to adapt to is his use of the same word 'beauty' for two apparently different functions of the mind[97]. But once we appreciate that the common element between the immediacy of incoming sensory effects and the immediacy of sensations or emotions that arise unbidden in our minds is their unmediated quality, then we can see his reasoning is faultless.

Both forms of 'beauty', as Shakespeare uses them, have an unwilled immediacy

---

[96] *Sonnet 125, as the penultimate Master Mistress sonnet, is explicit in rejecting the artistic excrescences of religion and society if they prevent the appreciation of the natural logic of love Shakespeare articulates throughout the sonnets:*

> Wer't ought to me I bore the canopy,
> **With my extern the outward honoring,**
> Or laid great bases for eternity,
> Which proves more short than waste or ruining?
> Have I not seen **dwellers on form and favour,**
> Lose all, and more by paying too much rent
> For **compound sweet; Forgoing simple savour,**
> Pitiful thrivers in their gazing spent.
> No, let me be obsequious in thy heart,
> And take thou my oblation, poor but free,
> Which is **not mixed with seconds, knows no art,**
> **But mutual render only me for thee.**
> > Hence, thou suborned *Informer*, **a true soul**
> > **When most impeached, stands least in thy control.** (*sonnet 125*)

[97] *We need only listen to John Keats conflate and confound truth and beauty in his famous 1820 poem 'Ode to a Grecian Urn' that celebrates a 'More happy love! more happy, happy love!' to get a measure of the problem admirers have had appreciating the beauty/truth/ beauty dynamic in Shakespeare's love sonnets:*

> '**Beauty is truth, truth beauty,** - that is all
> Ye know on earth, and all ye need to know.' (*Ode to a Grecian Urn, 49-50*)

and so are beyond judgment or approbation – hence outright 'beauty' is the appropriate word rather than downright 'black' or 'foul' as sonnet 127 explains. By calling both forms of sensation 'beauty' Shakespeare acknowledges the Greek understanding in which the aesthetic is any impression unmediated by thought[98]. Thought based in language occurs as a consequence of incoming sensations. It then creates and is informed by internal sensations of the mind. Both forms of sensation are singular effects – hence Shakespeare's insight that both can be represented by the same word, 'beauty'.

It seems Shakespeare is saying that deep and abiding love is most consistent and persistent for those who appreciate the isomorphic relationship between the physical grounds he lays out in the sonnet structure and mind-based possibilities he works into the female and male sequences[99]. He is suggesting – or claiming from his own experience in all likelihood with Anne Hathaway – that by basing his understanding in nature and the sexual dynamic (which are the grounds that determine the relationship of incoming sensations to the logic of language and the sensations or emotions of the mind) he is able to give his lively experience and understanding of love the deepest possible expression.

Shakespeare combines the treatment of truth as argument and beauty as poetry or art in the sonnets from 20 to 126. After examining truth in the previous section, in this section we have examined his analysis of beauty generated in the mind as a profoundly expressive condition for appreciating mature love.

---

[98] *If we use the word aesthetic to refer to any sensation whether externally induced or internally generated and use the word ethics to refer to any use of language with propositional intent in determining true and false, then we have Shakespeare's distinction between beauty and truth. To speak of truth otherwise is to miscall beauty truth – like Keats.*

[99] *See Conclusion below for a diagrammatic representation of the 154 sonnet isomorphism that maps the preconditions for Shakespearean love.*

12 The cost of misunderstanding love and hate

Have we reached the point in our unveiling of the logical structure of the sonnets where we can begin to consider profitably just why Shakespeare's understanding and expression of love proves so deeply moving and durable and so challenging to lesser evocations of love such as the Platonic or Christian or Romantic?

Now that we have examined both 'beauty' and 'truth' and 'truth and beauty', we might be able to better understand why some readers respond to the sonnets as if they are deeply religious, yet, as we are seeing, Shakespeare manages to incite those depths of emotion with a very earthy palette.

When we look again at the opening pair of sonnets that treat of truth and beauty for the Master Mistress, we find Shakespeare gives us all the clues we need to appreciate his deep insights into heightened emotional depths. A closer scrutiny of the logically joined pair 20/21 reveals that they differentiate between the natural 'beauty' available to the senses and the 'painted beauty' conjured in a mind inspired by an idealistic attitude to the youth's youth. Together sonnets 20 and 21 signal the Poet's intent in the following sonnets to address the relationship between everyday incoming sensory effects and the 'painted' effects to which the youth gives increased value because he is the incitement to idealised beauty.

We note that, besides differentiating first between truth and beauty and then the two types of beauty, both sonnets 20 and 21 mention 'love'. And again we find the Poet clearly distinguishing two types of love. He draws a clear distinction between the love he feels for the female compared to that for the male[100].

In sonnet 20 we hear the Poet reiterate the sexual dynamic to remind the Master Mistress of the foundation of his sensibility in the natural dynamic of female and male. He then differentiates between the love for a woman and that for a man. He states categorically the youth's body is created biologically to love a woman and the sign of that love is the youth's prick designed by 'nature' to fit the women's 'treasure' for 'women's pleasure'. In contrast, he accepts his love of the male youth is non-biologically or erotically of the mind for the mind.

The Poet reminds the youth of his biological relationship toward females (as argued in sonnet 9) and reconciles himself with the non-sexual or erotic masculine relationship of mind-to-mind/body-to-body. This is the love relationship celebrated in sonnet 116 where, if the youth matures sufficiently, he will enjoy the intensified emotion of a 'marriage of true minds' with the Poet and effectively with the encompassing mind of the Mistress' feminine and masculine personae.

---

[100] *The role of sonnet 20 in the set is pivotal for the transition from the love that is inherent in the sexual dynamic of increase to the fully realised potentiality of deeply affective love for all humankind. Shakespeare presents a clear understanding of love in his sonnets to rectify the compromised love encapsulated in the self-parodying eroticism of male-based myths:*

And **for a woman wert thou first created**,
Till **nature** as she wrought thee fell a doting,
And by addition me of thee defeated,
By **adding one thing to my purpose nothing**.
　But since she pricked thee out for women's pleasure,
　Mine be thy love and thy love's use their treasure. (*sonnet 20*, 9-14)

Better than that, the Poet directly critiques the forms of idealised love traditionally seen as superior – in particular, the love associated with a singular male God. As Shakespeare indicates in his sonnets (particularly 129 and 146) and explores in depth in his poems and plays, the love of such a God in practice leads to the most debilitating form of hate visited by humans on themselves.

We have observed that sonnet 20 sets the record straight about male-God creation by insisting that woman comes before man. Now we can watch as sonnet 21 emphasises Shakespeare's critique of the form of love engendered in the airy spaces of heaven rather than in the human dynamic in nature.

The Poet deprecatingly accepts that the type of 'Muse' who is 'stirred by a painted beauty to his verse' creates effects that a heaven could 'use' to its advantage. But, in contrast, the Poet claims his poetry, and hence his 'love', is as 'fair as any mother's child'[101]. This reference to the increase argument in nature is backed by the Poet's assertion that the 'heaven' cited by that Muse is supported by no more than 'hear-say'. Hence the Poet says he cannot 'praise' those who in the name of heaven have airy nothings to 'sell'.

There could not be a clearer statement of Shakespeare's appreciation that his verse is more than equal to that written in praise of an idealised love based in airy candle-stick heaven. By basing his understanding in nature, as evident in his deliberately structured sonnet set, the Poet exhorts his readers not to purchase dummy love.

When we look to other Master Mistress sonnets that inter-relate truth and beauty and religious sensibility, we recall that sonnet 66 very deliberately defines the Poet's understanding of 'truth' and compares it to the tendency to misrepresent idealistic affects in the mind by simplistically calling them 'truth'. Then in sonnets 67/68, immediately after sonnet 66, Shakespeare moves to examine the philosophic problem of confusing 'truth' with 'beauty'.

We find the sole subject of the two logically connected sonnets 67 and 68 (with a 'thus') that follow sonnet 66 is 'beauty' (with its associated 'Rose'). By reiterating the argument about beauty presented in sonnet 21 and looking ahead to the distinction between truth and beauty laid down in sonnet 101, sonnets 67

---

[101] *Sonnet 21 acts as the contractual counterpart to sonnet 20's statement of fact. As the natural conditions enunciated in sonnet 20 are self-evident, then the Poet need not and will not indulge in traditional metaphysical speculation:*

> Who **heaven** it self for ornament doth use,
> And every fair with his fair doth rehearse,
> Making a couplement of proud compare
> With Sun and Moon, with earth and sea's rich gems:
> With April's first born flowers and all things rare,
> That **heaven's air** in this huge rondure hems,
> **O let me true in love but truly write,**
> And then believe me, **my love is as fair,**
> **As any mother's child, though not so bright**
> **As those gold candles fixed in heaven's air:**
>> Let them say more that like of hear-say well,
>> **I will not praise that purpose not to sell.** (*sonnet 21*, 3-14)

and 68 examine explicitly the mind-based sensations the Poet refers to as 'beauty' in the Master Mistress sonnets.

In sonnet 67, the Poet calls the misunderstanding or the misrepresentation of beauty an 'infection' that is a 'sin' committed by those who take 'advantage' of the youth's idealisable mental attributes. Such 'false painting' imitates the youth's 'cheeks' (read both face and groin) and insinuates itself into his 'society'[102].

Then, in sonnet 68, the Poet calls the youth's 'cheek' – or sexual capacity – the 'map' of the days before the usurpation of female priority when 'beauty' was accepted as a sensation essentially similar to the singular sensations from 'flowers'. This was before the 'bastard signs of fair were born' or dared to inhabit a 'living brow'. So who is this 'bastard' born outside wedlock to assume the guise of a living being? The references to 'golden tresses of the dead', 'sepulchers', 'second life', 'dead fleece' (for Lamb of God) that follow the reminders of natural mapping make it clear that Shakespeare directs his critique at the mind-based compromise represented by the man-God Christ – who was born outside marriage seemingly of a virgin[103].

Again, the youth does not need to rob the 'old to dress his beauty new' as he is inherently a 'map' of 'Nature' that shows 'false Art what beauty was of yore'. Male-based ideologues have bankrupted the youth's 'nature' by inverting the natural dynamic so it seems nature now lives at the male God's behest. But 'nature', as both sonnets attest in their couplets, 'stores' the youth's potential in increase as was the

---

[102] *Sonnet 67 sets up the critique of 'false painting' by recalling a time when nature was not subverted by death-based 'infection':*
> Ah wherefore with **infection** should he live,
> And **with his presence grace impiety,**
> That sin by him advantage should achieve,
> And **lace itself with his society?**
> Why should **false painting imitate his cheek,**
> And **steal dead seeing of his living hue?** (*sonnet 67*, 1-6)
> ....
> O him she stores, to show what wealth she had,
> In days long since, before these last so bad. (*sonnet 67*, 13-14)

[103] *The map in sonnet 68 is the template out of which the idiosyncratic idealising youth can correct his inversion of truth and beauty:*
> Thus is his cheek the map of days out-worn,
> When beauty lived and died as flowers do now,
> Before these **bastard signs of fair** were born,
> Or durst inhabit on a living brow:
> Before the **golden tresses of the dead,**
> The **right of sepulchers,** were shorn away,
> To live a **second life on second head,**
> Ere **beauty's dead fleece** made another gay:
> In him those **holy antique hours** are seen,
> Without all ornament, it self and true,
> Making no summer of an other's green,
> **Robbing no old to dress his beauty new,**
> And him as for a map doth Nature store,
> To show false Art what beauty was of yore. (*sonnet 68*)

case before 'bad' male-based prejudice overthrew the 'wealth' of natural logic.

So here we have Shakespeare reiterating the grounds upon which he bases his sublime, mature and bountiful understanding of love. And, 400 years later, we can still hear his sonnets, plays and poems continue to finger the 'false art' behind the form of love that proffers so much but – as sonnets 67 and 68 attest and as predicted in sonnet 21 (and confirmed in sonnet 151) – is little more than a literary conceit played on the 'conscience' of humankind. Hence the perennial appeal of male-based prejudice to minds untutored in the mature love available in their birthright dynamic of truth and beauty.

We can get another measure of Shakespeare's awareness of the relationship between the idealistic religious love and the mature love he has gained from the Mistress by tracking the instances of the word 'dear' throughout the Master Mistress sonnets. What is the connection between the idealised or romantic love some think they find in Shakespeare's poems and plays and the mature love the sonnets reveal and how much does Shakespeare's mature love arise from his reflection on the 'airy' or 'costly' inadequacies of his own experience as a callow male youth?

The first realisation is that half the uses of the word 'dear' (10 of 21) and its derivatives – dearer/dearest (3 of 5) – question the 'cost' of adolescent idealism. In some of the other instances where 'dear' seems to express unguarded affection the meaning is equivocal.

We have seen that sonnet 31 proscribes 'dear (read 'costly') religious love'[104]. The critique is echoed on both sides of sonnet 31 with 'dear' and 'dearer' appearing in sonnets 30 and 32 respectively.

Then, scanning across the sonnets, we hear sonnet 48 talk of 'the best of dearest' and 'a prize so dear'. Sonnet 87 has 'thou art too dear for my possessing', sonnet 110 has 'sold cheap what is most dear (and mentions a 'God in love')'. Sonnet 117 has 'your own dear purchased right', and sonnet 122 has 'nor need I tallies thy dear love to score'.

So, there is little doubt Shakespeare distinguishes his nature-based love from the costly consequences of indulging in 'religious love' without circumspection. Here we have evidence for the contrary effect his love sonnets have on those who buy into religious love to the detriment of their natural understanding and emotions. Shakespeare's wording 'dear religious love' captures perfectly the attraction of his sonnets for those who take a sentimental reading of the phrase without hearing the criticism the phrase is designed to awaken in their overwrought faiths.

It is also instructive to track Shakespeare's use of the word 'soul', as many who seek resonances with their religious beliefs in the sonnets most likely mishear its significance in Shakespeare's critique of the ideal-driven confusion of truth for beauty. For instance, the double appearance of 'soul' in sonnet 146 leads believers to expect a rendering sympathetic to their male-based faiths.

---

[104] *Sonnet 31 makes no bones about where 'buried love doth live' (line 9):*
    How many a **holy and obsequious tear**
    Hath **dear religious love stolen from mine eye**,
    As **interest of the dead**, which now appear,
    But things removed that hidden in there lie. (*sonnet 31, 5-8*)

The first of the fourteen instances of the word soul appears as the plural 'souls' in sonnet 20 – after the givens of nature, female and male, and after the Poet establishes the prerequisites for increase and writing. In the first of the truth and beauty sonnets of the Master Mistress sequence, Shakespeare says that the youth, who was created for women, 'steals men's eyes' and amazes 'women's souls'. If there is a soul it lies in the nature-based dynamic of which women are the originary entities.

Then the soul is identified with 'thought' in sonnet 26 and with the imagination in sonnet 27. In sonnet 62 the 'soul' is possessed of the 'sin of self love', and in sonnet 69 it is associated with 'all tongues' that are 'the voice of souls' capable of uttering 'bare truth'. In sonnet 107, the 'prophetic soul' dreams 'on things to come' unable to control 'my true love' and sonnet 109 houses the soul in the youth's 'breast' rather than the 'wide universe'.

Shakespeare's understanding of the soul seems to mirror his understanding of the heart. They are metaphors for the seat of the ideals and the emotions respectively. This reading seems borne out by sonnet 125 where 'a true soul' in the religious sense stands 'most impeached' when it is not free – as the Poet's mature love is free – but is in the 'control' of the 'outward honouring' of religious or social 'form and favour'.

So, it appears that Shakespeare has little time in the Master Mistress sequence for the heavenly or extraterrestrial soul of religions – and this conforms with his rejection of such 'astronomy' in sonnet 14. As the Poet credits the first mention of 'souls' to women in sonnet 20 let us see how the beleaguered soul fares in the Mistress sequence.

In sonnet 136, the Poet uses the word 'soul' three times in the first three lines. He says that if the Mistress' 'soul' should 'check' the advance of his 'will' or penis as it comes 'so near', she 'knows' his 'will' is willing to be 'admitted' to her 'blind soul' that is her 'treasure' or vagina. Shakespeare is in no doubt that the path to the mind's soul is through the woman's 'nothing' that he, on her 'store's account' (or increase), should be at one in.

When we turn to the famous sonnet 146, we find the heavenly 'soul' is not held on high but lamented as a 'poor soul' that is the 'centre' of the Poet's 'sinful earth'. A 'large cost' (that association cost/dear again) is attributed to the soul that lives upon death by 'selling hours of dross'. After all, the couplet concludes, once 'men' are dead there's 'no more dying then'.

The last sonnet in the set to mention 'soul' is 151. This time the Poet's soul is accused of deceiving his body by playing off the supposed 'nobler part' against his 'gross body'. But in the Mistress sequence the Poet has learnt to recover his conscience by removing the guilt associated with religious 'love'. He laconically accepts his status as 'drudge' or male derived from female as he triumphantly regales her with a cascade of erotic verse[105].

---

[105] *Sonnet 151 deals decisively to the illusion of the immortal soul by locating 'conscience' in the natural dynamic of increase out of which mature love can rise – and fall:*
> **Love is too young to know what conscience is,**
> **Yet who knows not conscience is born of love,**

So, it seems Shakespeare's treatment of the noble 'soul' betrays not a regard for religious verities but an acceptance that the soul is ingrained in the human mind. He warns that biblical guilt clouds the human conscience. Instead, the love that arises out of nature and is spoken of in the increase sonnets is the source of conscience and is the basis for being 'contented'.

The double depth of the sonnets' treatment of love is also evident in the three instances in which the word 'God' occurs. Since beauty – as picturing, imaging and art – is associated so clearly with the tendency to overvalue ideal effects in the human mind, Shake-speare is quite exact in critiquing the instances where the male God commands precedence over the natural logic delineated in his 154 sonnets.

As we have seen, sonnet 58 specifically mentions the biblical male God and subjects his imaginary effects to the same critique as the more general critique of the male youth's idealism. In sonnet 58, Shakespeare cites the irony where the God of the bible enslaves the youth to an anti-increase obstinacy without acknowledging that the eroticism of his own mind-based genesis derives from the logic of increase in nature.

Then, in sonnet 110, we hear that the enslaving God morphs into a 'God in love'. The Poet recounts how he once ignored his own advice in sonnet 21 about praising those who sell heaven's air that is not there to be sold. He learns that the natural love inherent in youth – his 'older friend' – is a 'God in love' to whom he is naturally 'confined' in his own loving 'heaven'. Then, in sonnets 153 and 154, the 'God in love' becomes the 'little Love-God'[106] .

The inter-relationship from sensory 'beauty' through 'truth' to mind-based 'beauty' is a continuous and fluid dynamic that never ceases as external sensations impinge on the mind, ideas are generated in the mind and emotions and intuitions are evoked in the mind. Shakespeare lays down the natural sequence of relation-ships in his set of sonnets. The dynamic is self-adjusting as ideas that are thought and emotions that are experienced are continually mapped out of nature and then back on to nature – as sonnet 68 asserts.

Shakespeare, more than any other writer, though, is preeminently conscious of the influence of the style and form of external art works on the manipulable human sensibility. In the increase to poetry sonnets 15 to 19, he alerts his reader to the

---

Then gentle cheater urge not my amiss,
Lest guilty of my faults thy sweet self prove.
For thou betraying me, I do betray
My nobler part to my gross body's treason,
My soul doth tell my body that he may,
Triumph in love, flesh stays no further reason,
But **rising at thy name doth point out thee,**
As his triumphant prize, **proud of this pride,**
He is **contented thy poor drudge to be**
To **stand in thy affairs, fall by thy side.**
No want of conscience hold it that I call,
Her love, for whose dear love I rise and fall. (*sonnet 151*)

[106] *See footnote 25 for quotes.*

tendency to believe in creations of the mind such as the male God and immortality of the soul – especially as art works give them such a beguiling presence.

Shakespeare's principal criterion for evaluation is the relationship between the susceptibility of humans to idealised love, whether on the page or in artworks, and his own experience of mature natural love – putting aside his own exceptional talent as a poet and playwright. Whereas the effects of the two forms of 'beauty' in the mind are unavoidable they are also inherently debatable. But once they are reproduced as poems, plays or artworks they are frequently treated as infallible. It is then that they incite the inevitable love/hate syndrome amongst those who usurp nature with a 'Word'.

So Shakespeare has it both ways. He evokes a love consistent with the experience of love in all its depths by humans in nature and deconstructs the love that is the conditional love of the male God who inhabits the human mind. As he recalls in sonnet 145, the learning curve he underwent took him from such a God whose love in natural terms is a hate (as evident in the hate between religions who hold to such a male God exclusively) to regain the sense of love developed in nature as an expression of contentedness for all humankind.

Shakespeare clearly differentiates between his comprehensive and consistent nature-based love and other forms of love based in the human imagination. By developing his nature-based philosophy in a set of love sonnets he shows both the limitations of mind-isolated emotions and gives fulsome expression to his deeper and enduring mature love.

13 Why Shakespeare considers 'beauty' and 'truth' before 'truth and beauty'

Can we now say we understand why the female imparts 'beauty' and 'truth' separately and sequentially to the Poet while the Poet instructs the male in 'truth and beauty' concurrently? And what does it say of Shakespeare's philosophic acumen that he lays out the logic of 'beauty' and 'truth' and 'truth and beauty' by basing his understanding in palpable nature rather than imaginary Gods? Why are the two different arrangements so crucial for Shakespeare's expression of mature love?

To get some perspective on why 'beauty' and 'truth' are separated in the Mistress sequence and why 'truth and beauty' are not separated in the Master Mistress sequence we first recall that in the Mistress sonnets 'beauty' refers to incoming sensations from the world about.

As we probed deeper into both the Mistress and Master Mistress sequences we found further evidence that 'beauty' in the Mistress sequence refers to incoming sensations that are experienced unbidden in the mind. Significantly, Shakespeare's Poet makes an empirical assessment in sonnets 127 to 137 of the sensory effects the Mistress has on his organs of sight, hearing, smell, touch and taste. The Poet recognises that the primary sources of sensory input to the mind are externally observable and quantifiable.

In contrast, the language-based dynamic of thinking and speaking – which Shakespeare calls 'truth' in sonnets 137 to 152 – is generated primarily within the mind from those externally induced sensations. As Wittgenstein argues, the externally incited sensation of pain is first vocalized involuntarily as 'ouch' and then achieves verbal expression in the language game of pain.

So, in his organization of the twenty-eight Mistress sonnets Shakespeare first accommodates the crucial insight that externally sensory effects experienced as singular sensations in the mind ('beauty') differ substantially from the ensuing true/false dynamic of swearing or forswearing ideas ('truth'). This is because words in language represent sensations through socially agreed conventions – which Shakespeare calls the swearing and forswearing of oaths, vows, etc. Shakespeare shows that language is a social construct when he has the Mistress 'swear' and 'forswear' as she talks to the Poet in sonnets 138 to 152.

Shakespeare separates 'beauty' and 'truth' in the Mistress sequence because logically they represent different faculties of the mind. Significantly, when Shakespeare considers incoming sensations before language he is being biologically and hence logically exact. Biology and logic are inter-dependent because he bases his understanding of beauty and truth on the givens of nature and the female/male dynamic[107].

---

[107] *Shakespeare appreciates that only biological imperatives deserve ranking as logical givens. Because he knows that the logical systems of Aristotle and others are based on constructs engineered in human language he refuses to be beguiled by apparent logical 'truths' such as those represented as equalities: 1 + 1 = 2, or identities: God is good. Shakespeare's evident use of logical argument, based in nature and the sexual dynamic, in the structure of the 154 sonnet set and in groups and individual sonnets, plus his*

So Shakespeare's separation of 'beauty' and 'truth' in the Mistress sequence is a logical reflection of the natural distinction between external sensory effects and language generated in the mind through human intercourse. Because the female is inherently at one with nature and because the male is an offshoot of the female, it is only in her sequence that the logic of sensory effects from the world about is explained.

When we turn to 'truth and beauty' in the Master Mistress sonnets beginning at sonnet 20, Shakespeare is now effectively investigating the internal workings of the mind. The Poet continues the examination of the logic of truth begun in the second part of the Mistress sequence but now focuses more specifically on 'truth' as language, argument, writing, etc. And to complement the dynamic of 'truth' he adds mind-derived singular effects such as poetry, imagination and intuition that he also calls 'beauty'.

Hence, we can see that in the Mistress sequence the Poet learns and matures the basics of beauty and truth by first observing the Mistress and then listening to her talk until he turns the 'hate' engendered by his corrupt understanding of the mind into 'love'. Then, his principal task in the Master Mistress sequence is to instruct the male youth in the internal logic of the human mind to avoid mind-based delusions and excesses.

So, in the two sequences of the sonnet set we face two different modes of address. In the Mistress sequence there is the sensory and verbal give and take between two willing bodies/minds of the mature female and the maturing Poet. In stark contrast, in the Master Mistress sequence, there is no dialogue between the Poet and the adolescent male youth. Rather the Poet addresses a continuous stand-alone argument to the Master Mistress based on the intermix of 'truth and beauty'.

At no point does the Master Mistress engage in repartee with the Poet or even 'swear' as does the Mistress her sonnets – because effectively the Poet is retraining the masculine persona of the human mind, and so of his mind. Or, to put it another way, the Poet shows the Master Mistress the consequences of talking or swearing to oneself alone (as sonnet 131 forewarns). The subtext is that it is impossible to talk (or pray) to a male God because the mono-singular male God is a mental construct generated entirely by the conventions of language within the human mind.

And Shakespeare, as the consummate dramatist and poet, is well versed to have his Poet explain how language and the imagination are based in nature and the sexual dynamic of female and male. His Poet teaches the Master Mistress that while the internal workings of the human mind – with its continual interplay of sensations forming ideas and ideas forming sensations – is the most exciting of the mind's functions, it can also be the most confounding for any adolescent thinker/lover.

mocking of syllogistics in hilarious set pieces between secondary characters in some of the plays, is evidence of his refusal to indulge in mind-bending apologetics or logical mind-games. In Shakespearean logic, a tautology such as 'white is white' merely points to the failure to name a distinct sensation (beauty) – hence a tautology 'says' everything – and a contradiction such as 'white is black' points to a failure to represent a sensation in distinct language (truth) – hence a contradiction 'says' nothing – as Wittgenstein realised.

In contrast to the canny and cunning female who remains free of taste or favour, the male youth all too easily becomes a victim of the constructs of the human mind established through swearing. Shakespeare knows that the male will readily isolate himself psychologically if he succumbs to the mind-based 'self love' the Poet argues against in the increase sonnets.

Shakespeare's Poet is in no mood to equivocate as he lays down the logic of 'truth and beauty'. As we have seen, sonnet 66 very clearly differentiates between 'simple truth' and truth called 'simplicity' because truth is the dynamic of argument based on swearing and forswearing evident in thought, speech and writing. By having a clear appreciation of what he calls 'truth', Shakespeare achieves an unmatched veracity and maturity of understanding and love in his sonnets and his plays and poems. The quality of love they discuss is unmatched because he refuses to base his understanding of language on conceptual constructs generated purely in the mind.

But what really sets Shakespeare apart from every other poet and philosopher, is his unerring appreciation of the logic of sensations within the mind, which he also calls 'beauty'. First he acknowledges that, like the propositional dynamic of truth, poetic or artistic beauty is of the mind – hence, unlike the treatment of sensory 'beauty', artistic beauty cannot be independent of the mind. So the treatment of 'truth and beauty' in the Master Mistress sequence is concurrent.

Shakespeare's combined treatment of 'truth with beauty' (or ethics with aesthetics – in this case in the artistic sense) sets him apart as a thinker of great insight into human nature. It is the incisiveness of Shakespeare's insight that leads to his unrivaled clarity and depth of poetic and dramatic expression. By basing his understanding in nature and the sexual dynamic of female and male, and by writing the greatest dramas and love sonnets of their kind, Shakespeare shows he understands better than anyone before or since just how the effectiveness of poetry and art is generated and sustained.

Shakespeare's understanding of art makes his appreciation of 'beauty' and 'truth' and 'truth and beauty' more insightful than that of all the philosophers who apologise, if only by omission, for biblical prejudices. By identifying increase as the precursor for the possibility of love in nature (with its female/male dynamic) and then talking of love throughout his sonnets from the heart of the Mistress sequence to the soul of the Master Mistress sequence, Shakespeare both lays down the basic philosophy of truth and beauty and simultaneously accounts for our deepest experiences and expressions of love.

As we have seen, the Poet and the Mistress engage both body to body and mind to mind, whereas the Poet and Master Mistress engage primarily mind to mind. When the Poet shifts from the Mistress sequence to the Master Mistress sequence he delves deeper into the human mind because the 'addition' of the male increases the female potentiality – as sonnets 135/136 predict with their play on numbers and the double mention of 'store'.

Shakespeare bases his sonnet philosophy in both the biological relationship of female to male and the logical balance of feminine and masculine personae in the human mind. Shakespeare's greater concentration of sonnets to the male recognises that the mind-based dynamic of 'truth and beauty' is the one that controls human potential and contentedness. This explains why sonnet 116, with its recipe for 'the marriage of true minds', holds the key to resolving male-based intransigence.

And, in sonnet 116, Shakespeare summarises the logical conditions for mature love that arise from the complete dynamic he lays out in his 154 sonnets. The 'marriage of true minds' in the first line is not based on the shifting sands of ever-changeable pantheons of Gods but on the 'star' identified in sonnet 14 with the interrelationship between the sexual eye and the mind's eye. 'Love' cannot be measured by 'Time', or other mind-based conventions, but is intimately associated with the eroticism that devolves from the sexual dynamic in nature – as all myths bear witness.

We hear the interconnection between the sexual and the erotic when Shakespeare lyricises: 'though rosy lips and cheeks within his bending sickles compass come'. Then, recalling the prognostication of 'doom' in sonnet 14, the Poet asserts that, once there is a clear understanding of truth and beauty, the love engendered by the marriage of true minds 'alters not' even until the end of life if only because life continues through increase – with a pun in line 12 on 'bears' ~ 'bares'.

Shakespeare is so confident of his deep nature-based understanding and expression of love, in the couplet he avows that if it can be proved he is in 'error', then he accepts his poetry is as nothing and 'no man ever loved'. Shakespearean love based in nature, above style, rhyme and form, is the basis of all love, hence 'no man' has loved if the love laid out in the sonnets is in 'error'. As he does in sonnets 32 and 80, Shakespeare interconnects mature natural love that exists without words and its unprejudiced expression in words[108].

Here we have as good a reason as needed to claim that the logical arrangement of 'beauty' and 'truth' in the Mistress sequence and 'truth and beauty' in the

---

[108] *Sonnet 116 is rightly famous but for all the wrong reasons. Treated as a paean to absolute love, and hence as an expression of Christian love, or read at weddings to incite marital bliss, the sonnet is instead Shakespeare's statement of the requirements for achieving a mature love based in nature with its deeply embedded eroticism recognising the logical status of the sonnet as simply a vehicle for the Poet's love. As the couplet insists, it is an 'error' not to understand Shakespeare's generating philosophy and so misrepresent the quality of love the sonnet evokes:*

> Let me not to **the marriage of true minds**
> Admit impediments, **love is not love**
> **Which alters when it alteration finds,**
> Or bends with the remover to remove.
> O no, it is an ever fixed mark
> That looks on tempests and is never shaken;
> **It is the star to every wand'ring bark,**
> Whose worth's unknown, although his height be taken.
> **Love's not Time's fool, though rosy lips and cheeks**
> **Within his bending sickle's compass come,**
> Love alters not with his brief hours and weeks,
> But **bears** it out even to the edge of doom:
> **If this be error and upon me proved,**
> **I never writ, nor no man ever loved.** (*sonnet 116*)

Master Mistress sequence is both intentional and a precondition for appreciating and experiencing mature Shakespearean love. No wonder *Shakespeare in Love* loses the plot with its quiz-show word play, and little wonder daffodil Wordsworth was puzzle-pegged by Shakespeare's sweet and canker sonnets (sonnet 54) and sweet festering words (sonnet 94).

Shakespeare intentionally separates out incoming sensations from mind-based activities so making his sonnet set an exacting account of externally generated sensory impressions in relation to internally derived cognition and emotions. His philosophic clarity that incoming senses are distinct from mind-derived thoughts and feelings ensures the depth and consistency of Shakespearean love.

14 What the feminine and masculine says about the female and male

Can we begin to understand why Shakespeare introduces the logic of personae in the sonnets from sonnets 20/21 onward? And just why does he introduce the male into the female sequence and the female into the male sequence at specific locations two sonnets at a time?

At a few points in this essay we have noted instances where Shakespeare inter-relates the sexual dynamic of female and male and the gender dynamic of feminine and masculine. The evidence shows he infiltrates into the male and female sequences references to the Mistress and Master Mistress at localised hot spots in each other's sequences. So, is there a connection between 154-sonnet nature with its sexual division into two sequences of 28 female sonnets and 126 male sonnets and the apparent anomaly of the female appearing once in the male sequence and the male appearing twice in the female sequence?

We noted that the Poet introduces the gender relationship of feminine and masculine into the set in sonnet 20 when he calls the male youth the 'Master Mistress'. Up to that point, during the increase sonnets and sonnets 15 to 19, the Poet addresses the adolescent youth directly as a male. He argues to convince him as male of the logic of increase or 'husbandry' and the implications of increase for writing deeply affective poetry.

The shift from the physical function of increase to its ramifications for the mind is transacted in sonnets 15 to 19 with the pun on 'pen' in sonnet 16. But it is only in sonnets 20/21 that the Poet begins to instruct the youth in 'truth and beauty', or purely mind-based attributes. Hence, in sonnet 20, the name 'Master Mistress' captures the fact that the male derives biologically from the female and so besides having residual female bodily features he has feminine characteristics of mind.

But because the male is an offshoot of the female, then the name Master Mistress also invokes the originating gender dispositions of the female mind. So it seems Shakespeare takes into account both the sexual female/male dynamic and the shared gender dispositions of feminine and masculine personae for both female and male.

After this promising start we hear the Poet address the feminine/masculine dynamic specifically only three more times – in sonnets 41/42, 133/134 and 143/144. If the gender dispositions of the mind are a natural consequence of the sexual dynamic of female and male how does Shakespeare manage to write a set of sonnets in which there is a strong sense of feminine/masculine interplay – besides using the gender suggestivity of erotic language as does myth.

We know that when the Mistress instructs the Poet in beauty and then truth in sonnets 127 to 152, the Master Mistress appears in two sonnets in the beauty group and in two sonnets in the truth group. That Shakespeare includes the male in both the beauty and truth groups of the female sequence reinforces the female/male unity the Mistress represents. And the Mistress sustains her unity by maintaining the gender balance between feminine and masculine personae.

So, the appearance of the male in the female sequence means that the Mistress not only teaches the Poet the logic of beauty and truth, but also how to bring his gender relationship of feminine and masculine into balance. The Poet is then in a fit state of mind to instruct immature males (or overly masculinised females who neglect their feminine persona) in the conditions needed to attain unity.

From the evidence of the four sonnets in the female sequence that mention the male, the Mistress criticises or censures the Master Mistress without mercy. While, at first, the Poet seems to defend him, he then admits both the Master Mistress and he are but personae of the Mistress – albeit one adolescent and the other mature. We might expect, then, the two sonnets in the Master Mistress sequence that mention the Mistress to be critical of her. We find, though, that it is the male youth who is again at odds with the female's nature-based maturity – even to the point of rape as sonnet 41 recounts.

But, by the end of sonnet 42, we find the Poet rejoicing that the youth and he are one and hence the Mistress loves him 'alone'. The surprising unity after such interpersonal harm reflects the Poet's insistence that the male youth also represents the Poet's ineradicable memory of his youthful self-indulgence.

So, despite the apparent disunity of masculine to feminine, the masculine and the feminine personae always revert to a one to one partnership because of the stability of the biological givens of nature and the female/male dynamic. And as the nature-based Mistress encompasses both Poet and Master Mistress then together they constitute her complete persona.

Personae can be suppressed but not eradicated – no more than the basic logic of female and male for human life and love can be forgone. Hence, originary female/feminine nature always trumps male/masculine Gods despite commandments otherwise[109].

---

[109] *In her book 'Sexual Personae', Camille Paglia examines instances of sexual personae in literature and art down the ages. Not surprisingly she finds the literature and particularly the myths of every period full of colourful characters playing out gender roles. Even Shakespeare attracts her attention, but because she does not understand his nature-based sonnet philosophy she does not draw the crucial distinction between sex and gender and sex and eroticism as does Shakespeare. She overlooks the basis for gender in the sexual dynamic of female and male in nature and the gender constitution of the Gods and Goddesses of all religions including the biblical God. Worse, despite her willingness to discuss the sexual personae of mythic characters such as Christ and Mary, she is leadenly quiet on the gender constitution of the biblical God – whose usurpation of female priority identifies him as the most overly masculinised entity ever conceived in the human imagination. And tellingly, like many authors, she fails to give God an entry in her index despite frequent mentions of the word God in her text. Should we be surprised, though, when she joins those like Carl Jung who rail against nature. Despite Paglia's acceptance that 'Shakespeare's elemental energy comes from nature itself' (p.195), her ingrained prejudice against nature is evident when she sees in Cleopatra 'the untransformed energy of nature, sheer sex and violence' (p.217) and reflects that those who live on the 'land recognise nature's terrible amorality' (p.218). So, in complete contrast to the evidence of this essay where the adolescent male who is taken to task is the generic model for all the males and overly masculinised females in the plays, Paglia claims the 'androgynous' (p.205) boy of the sonnets 'belongs to the sonnets and must remain there' (p.206). Yet we have seen that Shakespeare views nature as relatively benign compared to the evil and hate engendered by male-based religions such the Italian Catholic – to which Paglia maintains an uneasy*

We need to stand back a little to see what this means. In the Master Mistress sequence we watched as the Poet argues that the headstrong youth's imbalanced male-based mind-derived ideals are at odds with natural logic or the prior status of the female for increase, love and understanding. Because the youth's physical characteristics are nature-given, the Poet's increase argument aims to correct the imbalance in the feminine and masculine disposition of the adolescent mind. So, contrary to centuries of prejudice that the early sonnets censure a young Lord for sexual laxity, the Poet is less interested in discouraging or encouraging youthful licentiousness.

After the increase argument that questions the youth's male-driven 'self love' and after the increase and poetry sonnets assert the logical dependence of verse on physical increase, we then see sonnets 20/21 reiterate those concerns and add the argument for an art based primarily in natural values rather than airy heaven-based ideals. So, all the Poet's 'best' (as sonnet 76 puts it) is spent teaching the youth how to turn 'hate' to 'love' (as sonnet 145 recounts).

An example of the process in reverse may help. In *Macbeth*, Shakespeare shows what happens when a male (Macbeth) and a female (Lady Macbeth) both blindside their feminine/masculine gender dispositions. At the play's start the love between Macbeth and his wife is unremarkable. It has not reached the point where their gender equations turn rancid and fester – as sonnet 94 warns. But when 'peerless Kinsman' Macbeth becomes 'Bellona's Bridegroom' and 'most kind Hostess'[110] Lady Macbeth vows to dash her babe's 'brains out', they both become doubly masculinised by completely denying their feminine sensibilities[111].

loyalty. In 'The Rape of Lucrece' Shakespeare clearly distinguishes between the 'faults' of nature that we all are born with and the completely avoidable products of mind-based 'infamy':

> For marks descried in **men's nativity**,
> Are **nature's faults, not their own infamy**. (*The Rape of Lucrece*, 538-9)

The two lines distinguish between unconscionable mind-based faults and readily mitigated 'faults' which occur in the general course of nature. The excerpt from the long poem is consistent with what we have seen of Shakespeare's nature-based philosophy. That Paglia is so determined to override Shakespeare's understanding by isolating the sonnets from the rest of his works is an indictment of her simplistic literary critique. (Camille Paglia, *Sexual Personae: Art and Decadence from Nefertiti to Emily Dickinson*, London, Penguin, 1991.)

[110] *Both assessments are made by God-fearing King Duncan whose simplistic mind-based idealism leaves him unable to anticipate either his own bloody death or evil in others.*

[111] *When, in the second scene of 'Macbeth', the 'bloody' Captain recounts his tale of war he sets the scene by invoking Christ's bloody moments on the cross:*

> Captain: Except they meant to bathe in **reeking Wounds**,
> Or **memorise another Golgotha**,
> I cannot tell: but I am faint,
> **My Gashes cry for help**. (*Macbeth*, 1.2.59-63)

Then, when the dependable Ross remarks that Macbeth outperformed himself in battle, he characterises his achievement as worthy of the Goddess of War's male consort Mars – 'Bellona's Bridegroom'. By naming Bellona rather than Mars, Shakespeare has Ross speak to Macbeth's martialised feminine persona:

Shakespeare argues in *Macbeth* that the consequence of male-based prejudice, represented archetypically by the biblical male God, is to instigate a double-headed tragedy. The male loses touch with his female origins and the female strips herself of her natural heritage – and it all originates in the human mind.

So we might expect Shakespeare to address a sustained argument in the sonnets against the imbalance that male-based excesses represent. When we look to the sonnet that follows sonnets 20/21 in the Master Mistress sequence, we find it compares the relationship between the youth's male-driven predicament and the Poet's recollections of his similar youthful experiences.

Shakespeare dedicates sonnet 22 to exploring the mind-based relationship between the 'youth' and the Poet's youthful self. Sonnet 22 announces immediately after sonnet 20/21 that the crucial issue is the maturation of the masculine persona. Because the Poet has experienced the level of immaturity he depicts in the male youth, he is in a position to instruct him with sympathy away from the debilitating excesses of adolescent male-based idealism toward mature love[112].

But, importantly, in the Master Mistress sequence, as the generic name for the male suggests, Shakespeare's Poet not only has the role as sonnet writer to mature the immature mind of the stubborn male who refuses to develop his feminine sensibility. Shakespeare also gives the Poet the role of correcting the overly masculinised mind of females who, like the father-afflicted Kate in *The Taming of the Shrew* and the God-afflicted Isabella in *Measure for Measure*, have

> *Ross:* Till that **Bellona's Bridegroom**, lapped in proof,
> Confronted him with self-comparisons,
> Point against Point, rebellious Arm 'gainst Arm,
> Curbing his lavish spirit: (*Macbeth*, 1.2.79-82)
>
> *Then we hear Lady Macbeth hope that 'no compunctious visitings of Nature' will 'shake' her 'purpose' (1.5.396-397), and a little later, to strengthen her unnatural resolve, she is willing to forgo increase and so the whole logic of human love and understanding:*
>
> *Lady Macbeth:* **I have given Suck**, and know
> How tender 'tis **to love the Babe that milks me**,
> I would, while it was smiling in my Face,
> Have **plucked my Nipple from his Boneless Gums**,
> **And dashed the Brains out**, had I so sworn
> As you have done to this. (*Macbeth*, 1.7.533-38)

---

[112] *Sonnet 22 poses a mirrorical double relationship between the mature Poet and the immature male youth and the mature Poet and his aged impressions of the residual effects of his own immaturity on his attained maturity:*

> My glass shall not persuade me I am old,
> **So long as youth and thou are of one date,**
> ....
> For all that beauty that doth cover thee,
> **Is but the seemly raiment of my heart,**
> **Which in thy breast doth live, as thine in me,**
> **How can I then be elder than thou art?**
> ....
>   Presume not on thy heart when mine is slain,
>   **Thou gav'st me thine not to give back again.** (*sonnet 22*, 1-14)

had their feminine personae alienated by male-based customs and beliefs.

The significance of the balance in feminine and masculine dispositions for mature understanding and love is shown by the continual examination of the inter-relationship of youthful and mature masculine personae throughout the sonnets. Sonnets 36, 39, 40, 42, 48, 58, 62, 88, 96, 104, 108, 109, 113 and 122 all celebrate the interconnectedness of the Poet and the Master Mistress both as separate sexual individuals and as gender aspects of the Poet's mind – and the youth's mind.

So, we now have a context for sonnets 41/42, 133/134 and 143/144. They extend the female or male individuality of the Mistress, the Master Mistress and the Poet to recognise the feminine and masculine personae inherent in the male Poet's mind – or that of a female Poet. And throughout the sonnets the dynamic of feminine and masculine personae is inherent in the minds of the Mistress and the Master Mistress and Poet.

We have noted the male appears twice in the female sequence but that the female appears in the male sequence just once. The pattern of the double male and single female appearances is another measure of the differing focus in the two sequences on beauty and truth. Shakespeare's deliberate interjection of the Mistress and Master Mistress so precisely into each other's sequences confirms the importance of his separation of 'beauty' and 'truth' in sonnet 127 to 152 and the intermixing of 'truth and beauty' in sonnets 20 to 126.

Hence, to recap, the Poet can only address the male youth logically if he accepts that as 'Master Mistress' or male he is derived from the Mistress or female – as sonnet 20 stipulates. Only if the youth acknowledges the Mistress' sensory immediacy, which we saw established in the first eleven sonnets of her sequence, can the Poet accost the male youth with any loving purpose.

But Shakespeare does not just rectify the inversion of female and male in biblical beliefs. While the physical status of female and male is basic to his nature-driven philosophy, he also examines the more pressing implication for the mind of the feminine/masculine gender relationship. What emerges from the insights into the dependence of mind-based personae on the female/male dynamic is that the mind is structured primarily according to gender dispositions and secondarily according to truth and beauty. And Shakespeare is pre-eminently aware of the interrelationship of both for a natural clarity of understanding and for achieving mature love.

To get an overview of Shakespeare's philosophic project we need to turn to a feature of the *Sonnets* not yet discussed. In *WSSP*, I present evidence that the famous dedication to the *Sonnets* is configured deliberately by Shakespeare to demonstrate the nature-based relationship between the persons of Poet, Mistress and Master Mistress and the feminine and masculine personae in the minds of either the male as Poet and Master Mistress or the female as Mistress.

The 28 dots in the body of the dedication can be seen to represent the female (in keeping with her 28 sonnets) and the initials 'T. T.' can be related to sonnet 126 with its unique form of six pairs of couplets. Both the structure of sonnet 126 and the name Thomas Thorpe replicate the number 126[113]. Hence the whole of

---

[113] *The coincidence that sonnet 126 is one sonnet with six rhymed couplets echoing the*

the dedication can be summed to represent nature as 154 or the total number of sonnets in the set. If we then sum the individual letters in the whole of the dedication we find there are 145 or the numbering for the Poet in the set[114].

TO.THE.ONLIE.BEGETTER.OF.

THESE.INSVING.SONNETS.

M'.W. H.   ALL.HAPPINESSE.

AND.THAT.ETERNITIE.

PROMISED.

BY.

OVR.EVER-LIVING.POET.

WISHETH.

THE.WELL-WISHING.

ADVENTVRER.IN.

SETTING.

FORTH.

T. T.

The dedication, then, represents both nature and the sexual dynamic of female and male (in the correct relationship of priority) and the personae of the feminine and masculine in the Poet's mind. And, as the Poet is the representative human who has matured his understanding and emotions, the complete contiguity of persons in nature and personae in the mind that Shakespeare figures into the dedication holds for any human being so achieved – female or male.

A further indication of Shakespeare's intentional configuration of the dedication comes when we consider the notorious pair of initials 'Mr. W. H.'. As 'W' and 'H' are the first and ninth letters in 'WILLIAM SHAKESPEARE' (as the name

---

sonnet number 126 and Thomas Thorpe is one name in two parts of six letters each also forming 126 is hard to ignore.

[114] *The connection of the Poet to the number 145, besides being based on the number of letters in the whole dedication, is evident in the playful rearrangement of numerals of nature's 154 to form 145. The simpler 145 suggests that, while the Poet is at one with nature, his understanding of nature's complexity is never commensurate. The role of number 145 is evident in sonnet 145, which is significant for the Poet's hate-to-love maturity, and can also be seen in the introduction of the 'I' (as Poet) in sonnet 10, 145 sonnets from the end of the set (see 'WSSP').*

appears under the title of *A Lover's Complaint*) then Shakespeare claims he has combined the unity (as 1) of the Mistress with the lack of unity (as 9) of the Master Mistress to achieve unprecedented depth of understanding and maturity in love.

The implication of Shakespeare's organisation of the dedication to interrelate persons and personae is that the whole set of sonnets can be read simultaneously in terms of female and male persons and feminine and masculine personae. So the insertion of the male in the female sequence and the female in the male sequence and the Poet's awareness of the youth as a person and as a persona merely confirm the much more significant understanding that *Shakespeare's Sonnets* of 1609 seamlessly combine persons and personae. Their interchangeability gives the set of 154 sonnets their amazing veracity and expressiveness for both understanding and love.

More significantly, by basing his philosophy in nature and by appreciating that the sexual dynamic of female and male gives rise to the gender dynamic of feminine and masculine personae, Shakespeare also accepts that all forms of human sexuality and genders dispositions are a possible consequence of human biology. This means the love so attractive to so many differing mind-sets is indeed available in Shakespeare's sonnets – and his poems and plays – without prejudice or judgment, so long as natural prerogatives are accepted.

Shakespeare simultaneously accounts for the female/male sexual dynamic in the structure of the complete set and the derivative gender feminine/masculine dynamic within the structure of the set. By acknowledging the logical interrelationship between female and male and feminine and masculine, Shakespeare puts conceptual backbone into the appreciation of mature love.

15 Love's cure in the erotic sonnets 153 and 154

What is the consequence for understanding and expression if the sexual dynamic in nature determines the constituents of the mind that Shakespeare itemises as incoming sensations, language use and emotions internal to the mind? How does he reconcile the logical influence of the sexual dynamic in nature with heightened emotions and sublime ideals?

Until now we have left out of our account of Shakespearean love the last two sonnets of the Mistress sequence, the most erotic sonnets of the set. Sonnets 153 and 154 are in a classical epigrammatic style but they are thematically part of the set with both mentioning the words 'mistress', 'eye' and 'love'.

Why should Shakespeare resort to style just when he has spent 152 sonnets establishing the basis for human love that avoids the conventions of 'rhyme' and 'style', especially the most basic stylistic creation of enthroning the male over the female in the heavenly misogyny endemic in biblical faiths?

But then we find that Shakespeare's use of a Roman epigram is not a simple borrowing of style. He takes the first few lines of a traditional conceit and extends it to provide a corrective to beliefs that prioritise the word over the flesh or the mind over the body.

We have seen how Shakespeare corrects the male-driven illogicality in Ovid's version of the story of Venus and Adonis. We have commented on the way he borrows and corrects conceits from biblical sources in *Measure for Measure* and *Twelfth Night, or, What you Will* and can show how he borrows and corrects from the plots of other authors for most of his thirty-six *Folio* plays to bring the original illogicalities into line with his natural logic in the comedies or demonstrate how the illogicalities lead to avoidable mayhem and death in the histories and tragedies.

Then there is the evidence from the 154-sonnet set that recovers a nature-based understanding with the female restored to her rightful place in relation to the male and increase validated for human survival. The God of religion turns into a 'God in love' and the costly consequences of 'dear religious love' are rejected. All these considerations, and others we have touched on, are brought to focus in the final two sonnets.

So, in what sense are the last two sonnets exemplary uses of Shakespeare's sonnet logic, which shows how to critique stylistic conventions? We note that the myths of the Bible are erotic stories of origins in that no character created in Genesis (Adam and Eve or even God) or in Christ's immediate family in the New Testament is born of natural increase. Consistent with births in all other myths of origin world-wide, they are born ex nihilo, out of clay, from a spare rib, from a virgin, or any non-sexual procedure from the birth-suite of the imagination.

Then, when we factor in the critique of male-based religions in the sonnets and plays, we can see that the last two sonnets foot-light the logic of the sonnet set by emphasising the erotic logic of all understanding because all understanding derives from the sexual dynamic in nature. Shakespeare's modification of the Roman epigram diverts its concern with the mal-consequences of illicit sex into an examination of the 'men'-driven 'maladies'[115] and 'men diseased'[116] religions that pervert the logic of increase and instead prioritise the erotic logic of the mind over a natural appreciation of 'truth and beauty'.

Being Shakespeare, he goes further in explaining somewhat sardonically why the verses of 'better' poets (sonnet 32) do not have the range and depth of his poetry and drama. If the beauty/truth/beauty dynamic is derived from and logically influenced by the sexual dynamic in nature, then the functions of the mind should be coloured by that influence.

Hence Shakespeare recognizes that the eroticism inherent in language – as witnessed in the art that is myth – is the marker that signals the source of language in the sexual dynamic. So not only are the last two sonnets intensely erotic to celebrate that realisation, throughout the sonnets that address beauty/truth/beauty there are frequent passages whose erotic references signal the fundamental erotic characteristic of language out of nature.

When we scan the 154 sonnets we find that the increase sonnets avoid erotic innuendo. Their argument for the logic of increase is deliberately literal and prosaic. Next, the increase and poetry sonnets use a single erotic pun on pen/penis as befits their role as transitional sonnets between increase and poetry or between the body and the mind.

The sea change occurs in sonnets 20/21 and continues in the remaining sonnets devoted to truth and beauty in both sequences. When we enter the human mind through the sense organs in the early Mistress sonnets, and explore truth and beauty in both sequences, the Poet uses sexual innuendo frequently to jet his meaning into

---

[115] *Sonnet 153 twice identifies the source for the cure of male-based maladies as the 'mistress' eye'. Both instances are in the singular making it apparent that a return to the logic of the female/male dynamic is required for perpetual love. Editors who change the 'eye' in line 14 to 'eyes' destroy the effect of the recovery of female priority during the previous 152 sonnets that leads to this moment of heightened common sense:*

> And grew a seething bath which men yet prove,
> **Against strange maladies a sovereign cure:**
> But at **my mistress' eye love's brand new fired,**
> The boy for trial needs would touch my breast,
> I sick withal the help of bath desired,
> And thither hied a sad distempered guest.
>   But found no cure, **the bath for my help lies,**
>   Where *Cupid* got new fire; **my mistress' eye.** (*sonnet 153, 7-14*)

[116] *Sonnet 154 celebrates the erotic power of verse based in the sexual dynamic:*

> And so the General of **hot desire,**
> **Was sleeping by a Virgin hand disarmed.**
> **This brand she quenched in a cool Well by,**
> Which from love's fire took heat perpetual,
> Growing a bath and **healthful remedy,**
> **For men diseased,** but I my Mistress' thrall,
>   Came there for cure and this by that I prove,
>   Love's fire heats water, water cools not love. (*sonnet 154, 7-14*)

minds of others configured as they are by the sexual dynamic in nature[117]

The Poet's acceptance of the erotic logic of language and internal mind-based sensations and emotions reaches a crescendo in the erotic intensity of Cupid's sonnets, 153 and 154. So, in our exploration of Shakespearean love we follow the Poet as he travels from the literal increase sonnets where love if selfish is murderous to the two final sonnets where love enters literature and begets the erotic dimension, which becomes disembodied in the mind-Olympics of biblical myths.

Even better, Shakespeare recognizes that because the sexual activity in all myths is erotic rather than biologically sexual, then all male-based myths, when they invert the natural female to male partnership, acknowledge their rootedness in nature and the sexual dynamic. By refusing to obey the convention cast in stone by Moses against questioning the erotic logic of the biblical myths, Shakespeare recovers the right to use the erotic logic of language without compromise. He breaks with every other apologetic philosopher over the last 4000 years who has justified – or not questioned – fundamentalist biblical prejudices.

Shakespearean love remains free of 'style' and 'rhyme' because Shakespeare rejects the stylistic convention of the priority of the male-God and simultaneously rejects the conventions of apologetic biblical writing or 'rhyme'. Instead he bases his understanding and hence his mature love in the givens of nature and the sexual dynamic of female and male.

The consequence is that the trajectory from the selfish love challenged in the increase sonnets and tracked through the remaining sonnets reaches its climax in the final two sonnets. The Ur-shift from the slave-making male God of sonnet 58 to the potential 'God in love' of sonnet 110, to the 'little Love-God' of sonnet 154 is complete. Contrary to the pejorative dismissals of sonnets 153 and 154 as Shakespeare's admission he contracted a sexually transmitted disease, the final two sonnets celebrate the recovery of mental health with an acceptance of the natural dynamic from the sexual to the erotic.

In contrast, the mythic God of the Bible and his son Christ, by their unnatural births, are unconscionably erotic and irredeemably bemired in the diseased closet of denial and retribution that follows on the conversion of natural love and hate to merciless mind-induced love/hate. Shakespeare more than any writer shows the way out of the black-box of 'sad distempered' conceits, sworn for reasons of self aggrandisement and power rather than for the love of humankind.

Ironically, because Shakespeare bases his understanding in the givens of nature and the female/male dynamic already established in the overall structure of the 154 sonnets, he uses the same logical components as those who write at a mythic level of expression. Shakespeare's uniqueness is that he writes at a mythic level without succumbing to the products of his own lively imagination. He escapes because he can see the irony. Hence the maturity of love we feel in his works is

---

[117] *We can compare Shakespeare, who bases his philosophy in the logical givens of female and male in nature to Kant, who has to resort to the mind-based conventions of time and space to structure his philosophy. Kant is unable to access the unconditional givens of female and male because they are compromised by his continued adherence to remnants of male-based myth. Hence his writings are not philosophy but apologia for illogical beliefs.*

deeply mythic without the compromises of male-based usurpation of female priority.

The evidence for Shakespeare intentionally structuring his arguments to the male youth around 'truth and beauty' rather than the usual focus on the conceits of time,[118] immortality,[119] etc., shows itself again and again as we delve into the sonnet complexity. Our argument is that only by following Shakespeare's lead can we plumb the depths behind his experience, understanding and expression of mature love.

So, in contrast to the apologetic philosophers who, with bedazzling disingenuousness, do not invert the male-God usurpation of female priority[120], Shakespeare not only corrects the illogicalities of human/God self love, he gives fulsome and sublime expression to the love inherent in his clear vision of humankind in nature. By publishing his philosophy in a set of love sonnets, Shakespeare simultaneously sets out his natural logic with its trajectory from nature to mind and gives it an expression which demonstrates his responsiveness to mature love and understanding.

Just as we react with emotion to those things we see in the world about, so too do we experience emotions in the deepest recesses of our minds. The love Shakespeare is justly renowned for runs the gamut from basic sensations that please the eye to the constructed art works that deliberately evoke spiritual and sublime mind-based responses.

Shakespeare recognises the distinction between the sexual and the erotic by making the presentation of the givens of nature and female/male and the logic of increase very prosaic and the sonnets that present truth and beauty deeply erotic. Appreciating the logical connection between the sexual dynamic of female and male and the erotic expression of language and art increases the expressive intensity of Shakespearean love.

---

[118] *In his commentary on the sonnets, John Kerrigan suggests that 'time' is the principal entity and gives capital Ts to every instance of the word time to make the sonnets conform to his prejudice.* (John Kerrigan, *The Sonnets and A Lover's Complaint*, London Penguin, 1986.)

[119] *Blair Leishman's preferred reading of Christian-like immortality in the sonnets runs foul of what he disparagingly calls Shakespeare's 'unplatonic hyperbole' as the nature-based sonnets refuse to bow to his male-based prejudice.*

[120] *The list of philosophers is as long as the reign of apologetics that justifies supplanting a male-God in place of the female priority in nature. They include Plato, Augustine, Aquinas, Descartes, Spinoza, Hume, Hegel, Kant, Schopenhauer, Nietzsche, Russell, Wittgenstein, and many others.*

16 Why does Shakespeare claim love is the basis of his poetry

When Shakespeare's Poet asserts his poetry will be remembered for its 'love' rather than for its 'style' or 'rhyme', can we now characterise the quality of love conveyed by Shakespeare's sonnets and plays that distinguishes it from all other writing? And what does Shakespeare predict will happen when his philosophy is understood?

Darwin devoted the first part of his *The Descent of Man and Selection in Relation to Sex* to explaining the derivation of human 'mental powers' and 'moral sense' through the evolutionary process. But as David Loye points out, besides mentioning the word 'moral' dozens of times Darwin also mentions 'love' ninety five times. This is in contrast to just two mentions of 'survival of the fittest'[121]. After describing the basic biology of species prior to our own in *The Origin of Species*, in *The Descent of Man* Darwin adds morals and love as crucial to the evolutionary survival of humankind.

This essay suggests Shakespeare's nature-based philosophy – which shows how to attain unmatched depths of love by respecting natural prerogatives – anticipates by 250 years and exceeds Darwin's understanding of the natural dynamic of love. Although Darwin wrote extensively in Parts 2 and 3 of *The Descent of Man* on erotic by-play, the implications of the mind-based emotions expressed in mythic poetry and art for mature love passed him by because, as he admitted, he was pre-occupied primarily with scientific pursuits.

Whereas Darwin simply describes the phenomenon of love from the evolutionary evidence, Shakespeare gives poetic expression to the logic of love. He maps logically the inter-connections from nature through the sexual dynamic of female and male and increase into the human mind and art, to evince in us the deepest possible feelings.

Shakespeare not only orders correctly the sequence of evolutionary priorities that lead to the capacity for humans to love the way they do, he writes verse in which he makes the deep sensation of love palpable for his readers. Shakespeare knew his sonnets would prove effective in transmitting his experience of love to generations of sonnet lovers.

We can see in sonnets 32 and 80 particularly that Shakespeare shows his consciousness of the exceptional power of his verse. In sonnet 32, where Shakespeare evokes his one 'Muse' needed to complete the nine of old – as sonnet 38 asserts – his Poet twice advises the youth that his 'poor rude lines' may well be 'out-stripped' in 'rhyme' or 'style' by 'better' poets. Instead, he claims his poetry will be 'read' and remembered for its 'love'[122].

---

[121] *David Loye, in 'Darwin's Lost Theory of Love' is the first scholar to listen comprehensively as Darwin takes account of the contribution of the human mind to the species' evolutionary advances.*

[122] *Sonnet 32 is adamant poetic talent alone does not guarantee verse enlivened by emotion:*

> And **though they be out-stripped by every pen,**
> **Reserve them for my love, not for their rhyme,** (*sonnet 32, 6-7*)
> *And in the couplet the Poet asks the youth to talk of him in these terms:*

In sonnet 80, from the heart of the alien Poet sonnets (78 to 86), the Poet plays mute in the face of the others' forthrightness, which is satirized erotically by Shakespeare as 'goodly pride'. If the Poet's verse remains unheard because he is 'tongue-tied', he can say unequivocally his 'decay' is a consequence of the maturity of his love[123]. And we have seen how, near the end of the Master Mistress sequence, sonnet 125 continues the theme with its criticism that 'form and favour' undermine mutual love.

Shakespeare's words have proven prophetic. In 400 years, despite many admiring his rhyme and style, none have plumbed the depths of his nature-based philosophy to reveal the quality of love they sense in his sonnets and in his poems and plays. In essence Shakespeare is saying he treats the 'worthier pen's' ability with rhyme and style as an elementary level of formulaic writing, while he reaches well beyond the conventions of poetry to engage directly with the reader's deepest feelings of love.

Besides the individual sonnets in which Shakespeare predicts the survival and effectiveness of his emotive verse, he appends the group of nine alien Poet sonnets to the centre of the set. They are aimed at a 'refined' Poet – or Poets – who specialise in 'style' and 'rhyme' and 'rhetoric' and with whom Shakespeare contrasts his poetry based in 'love'. Sonnets 78 to 86 criticise the youth for his willingness to accept the other's fatuous praise. Although their verse is admittedly competent, the youth remains resolutely immature if he claims for the same insubstantial reasons to admire or love the Poet and his verse.

The Poet emphasises the difference between the 'better spirit' and himself. He refuses to flatter the youth – despite their deep friendship. Instead he argues vigorously with him to establish the grounds for enduring love. If the youth is still blind to the patient explanation of the sonnet logic then the Poet is prepared to resign himself to silence and await the verdict of others down time[124].

> But since he died and Poets better prove,
> **Theirs for their style I'll read, his for his love.** (*sonnet 32*, 13-14)

[123] *In Sonnet 80 the Poet refuses to praise the youth for the sake of praise*:
> O how I faint when I of you do write,
> Knowing **a better spirit doth use your name**,
> And in the praise thereof spends all his might,
> To **make me tongue-tied speaking of your fame.** (*sonnet 80*, 1-4)

The Poet's mock of other Poets ability to praise ends with a tongue-in-cheek avowal in the couplet of the maturity of love evident in his verse:
> Then if he thrive and I be cast away,
> **The worst was this, my love was my decay.** (*sonnet 80*, 13-14)

[124] *When editors attribute parts of plays to other playwrights such as Fletcher and Middleton, and when they treat the 154 sonnets as a biographical resource or at best as evidence that Shakespeare based his understanding in the biblical or classical traditions, they do so because they are ignorant of the sonnet philosophy. The difference between Shakespeare and his contemporaries and predecessors is in the consistent and comprehensive philosophy he articulates in the 154 sonnets. As competent as Fletcher and others might have been as playwrights, they did not have Shakespeare's oversight that*

If we take the arrangement of the Master Mistress sequence at face value, then the Poet's criticisms of the male youth identify precisely the stylistic constraints that keep the poetry of other Poets from achieving his unfettered expression of love. The most telling challenge is to the convention of placing the male before the female in biblical beliefs[125].

Effectively, any understanding and expression that prioritises a male God over the female or nature reveals its stylistic origins in its impermanence and unbelievability. The succession of religions over the last 4000 years and the non-universality of belief in any one God are in stark contrast to the ubiquity of nature and the sexual dynamic for millions of generations of human beings.

So, by structuring the natural priority of the female over the male into his sonnet set, Shakespeare identifies the inversion of the male over the female as the primary stylistic conceit that leads to putting God before nature, time before nature, self before nature (and increase), which in turn leads to poetry that lacks the integrity and depth of his mature verse. His criticism, then, is of the systems of thought and belief – rather than individuals – that enforce such unnatural expectations of love by basing their appeal on fear and hate for a temporary gain in power.

Shakespeare's treatment of rhyme also challenges the desire in other writers to achieve perfect rhymes. *Shake-speares Sonnets* (*Shakespeares* has no apostrophe in Q) of 1609 are notorious for their mis-rhymes, for lines of rhythmic complexity and for sonnets that do not conform to the regular pattern such as 99 with its extra line, 126 with its rhyming couplets and 145 in octosyllables.

The compulsion of most editors of the sonnets to correct Shakespeare's deliberate mistakes shows up their misunderstanding of his appreciation of love based in nature where the conventions of poetry act as mere window-dressing[126]. Instead,

---

allowed him to present in deeply philosophic poetry the logic behind all his long poems and plays. Like Marcel Duchamp in the twentieth century, who set down the logical conditions for any mythic expression in his 'Large Glass' and 'Notes' as the basis for his other art works – and by implication for all art works, Shakespeare not only successfully presents the philosophy behind his own works, in doing so he magisterially contextualizes all other authors and artists past and present within the ambit of his unprecedented and unequalled insights and emotive awareness. No wonder editors like Gary Taylor and his bevy of academic dogsbodies flounder around the edges of Shakespeare's achievement. Without the philosophy of the sonnets to guide them they are powerless and rudderless in the slipstream of their own ignorance.

[125] *The twentieth-century artist Marcel Duchamp most nearly approaches Shakespeare's achievement of avoiding stylistic and formulaic constraints on his art works. Duchamp talked of getting 'beyond taste' and said he would call a movement based on his example 'eroticism'. Like Shakespeare, Duchamp corrects the usurpation of female priority by male-based prejudice in his two major works 'The Bride Stripped Bare by Her Bachelors, Even' and 'Etant donnes'. By correcting the deepest of the stylistic constraints, Duchamp produced a body of work that was consistent, inventive and influential. But whereas Shakespeare's critique and expression of eroticism and love is comprehensive of all the human faculties, Duchamp limited his activities to art.*

[126] *A lack of understanding of Shakespeare's philosophy, with its extraordinarily natural*

we find that Shakespeare not only allows such seeming mistakes to remain, he gives them a freight of meaning as part of his intricate structuring and numbering of the sonnets.

In the face of the excessive rhetoric of the 'worthier' pens in praising the external beauty of the youth, Shakespeare accuses them of taking advantage of the youth's susceptibility to false praise. He echoes the tendency of male-based religions to gain adherents by misrepresenting the status of nature, and states his preference to remain silent rather than have his deeply philosophic intentions misinterpreted by the youth and used unfairly against him.

Altogether, then, Shakespeare's appreciation that his love sonnets will stand the test of time because he refuses to conform to stylistic conventions plus his criticism of those who do abuse nature with their undeliverable conceits gives his set of sonnets qualities that both attract those seeking deep love and repel those who have compromised their natural heritage. And, as Wordsworth demonstrates, both attraction and repulsion can affect the same person.

Shakespeare rejoices quietly in his ability to both inculcate into his sonnets the deepest form of love and to structure his set of 154 sonnets to demonstrate just how he was able to write verse that does so.

Shakespeare uses the word 'content' in the first sonnet to capture the peace of mind associated with his appreciation of the natural dynamic of love. He accuses the niggard youth of burying his 'content' within his youthful 'bud'[127]. Shakespeare's concern for the youth's 'content' is double-sided. He sees the male youth refusing to acknowledge the content of his deeply philosophic verse and so missing out on the possibility of deep contentedness and love.

Sonnet 55 explicitly identifies the 'contents' of the Poet's verse with the

---

heights of love, has led to the many quibbles and foibles by those charged with editing and commentating on his works for the last 400 years. How ironic then that those who approach the sonnets with Christian, Romantic, Platonic, or any other mind-set find that while a few of the sonnets such as 18, 116, 129, 146, etc., (usually emended) can be made to conform to their expectations, other sonnets seem harsh and contrary. But Shakespeare's understanding and expression of love is based on a completely consistent and comprehensive philosophy which, when understood, validates the deep natural empathy many have experienced in front of his works. In contrast, the film 'Shakespeare in Love' represents the worst misreading of Shakespeare's works when it substitutes the convention of a hypothesised London mistress for the deep love Shakespeare experienced with Anne Hathaway. Worse it crafts the supposed love mistress out of a simplistic reading of the women from Shakespeare's own plays when his mature love gained in his relationship with Anne is more than sufficient to explain the qualities the women exhibit in his poetry and plays. As Germaine Greer argues from the evidence of Elizabethan/Jacobean social conditions, there is every reason to believe Anne Hathaway was a competent woman in her own right, deeply committed to Shakespeare and possibly instrumental in the publication of the 1623 'Folio'.

[127] *The first sonnet of the set not only identifies increase as a significant issue it relates the potential to be 'content' to increase:*
  Within thine own bud buriest thy **content**,
  And tender churl mak'st waste in niggarding: (*sonnet 1*, 11-12)

philosophy he articulates in the sonnets[128]. The 'contents' in which the Master Mistress will 'shine more bright' than 'the guilded monument of Princes' involves the 'living record of your memory…even in the eyes of all posterity'. The 'ending doom' of line 12 is the same 'doom and date' warned of in sonnet 14 if the logic of 'store' or increase is voided. And when the Poet says the youth will 'live in this' he means in the 'contents' – mentioned in the first sonnet and defined by the whole set of sonnets.

A little later, in sonnet 74, Shakespeare makes the connection between being 'contented' and the contents which the Poet's verse 'contains'[129]. The Poet recalls the double meaning of the word 'line' that he invokes in sonnet 18 where lines of life and lines of poetry come together. So the 'this' in the couplet is indeed what the sonnet 'contains' – instead, the Poet's death leaves his body the 'prey of worms'. In contrast, increase – and the understanding of truth and beauty consistent with its logic presented in the 154-sonnet set – 'remains' with the Master Mistress as his birthright.

And a search through the plays shows that Shakespeare uses the word content in some context in all the plays. Shakespeare does not offer the moralistic goal of Utilitarian happiness but a contentedness that follows an understanding that corrects all the prejudices and injustices of anti-nature and anti-female religions. His plays are a devastating criticism of the lack of natural content and contentedness in the syndrome that blights those faiths.

---

[128] *Sonnet 55 interrelates the impermanence of human monuments with persistence through 'posterity' that enables the Poet to write verse in which the 'contents' are palpable and irreducible to 'powerful rhyme':*

Not marble, nor the guilded monument,
Of Princes shall out-live this powerful rhyme,
But you shall shine more bright in these contents
Than unswept stone, besmeared with sluttish time.
When wasteful war shall *Statues* overturn,
And broils root out the work of masonry,
Nor *Mars* his sword, nor wars quick fire shall burn:
The living record of your memory.
'Gainst death, and all oblivious enmity
Shall you pace forth, your praise shall still find room,
Even in the eyes of all posterity
That wear this world out to the ending doom.
  So till the judgment that yourself arise,
  You live in this, and dwell in lovers' eyes. (*sonnet 55*)

[129] *Sonnet 74 connects the contentedness the Poet inculcates into his verse with the true 'worth' of 'that which it 'contains':*

But **be contented** when that fell arrest,
Without all bail shall carry me away,
My life hath **in this line** some interest,
Which for memorial still with thee shall stay.
  ….
  The worth of that, is that which it contains,
  And that is this, and this with thee remains. (*sonnet 74*, 1-14)

Whereas the intellectual adventure of understanding the philosophy of Shakespeare's *Sonnets* can make the individual sonnets seem transparent, once the philosophy is interrelated with their palpable expression of mature love the effect is to dissolve the sonnet set leaving an emotional and intellectual experience of the promised 'contents' and contentedness of human life and love in nature.

Shakespeare acknowledges that the quality of his sonnet writing alone is not sufficient for mature love – rather the ability of his 154-sonnet set to represent the trajectory from nature through human understanding to deeply felt human love stands them apart. Fully comprehending the deep meaning of love in life and art is essential for gaining penetrating insights into the experience, understanding and expression of mature Shakespearean love.

17 Conclusion: love, but only as we know it

Can we now visualize a philosophic 'map' for love embodied deliberately in the sonnets to better appreciate the brilliant simplicity and veracity with which Shakespeare is able to evoke our deepest emotions with unmatched vivacity for our mature experiences and expectations of love?

Again, we might ask why Shakespeare's sonnets are regarded near universally as the greatest love sonnets in English literature or any literature. And what makes *Romeo and Juliet* the most famous play about star-crossed lovers? So, how to explain the deeply affective expression of love Shakespeare infuses into his works?

Can we begin to understand why Wordsworth is attracted one minute and repulsed the next when he reads about love in the sonnets? And have I accounted for my apprehension that *Shakespeare in Love* cheats and cheapens by suggesting Shakespeare got it all from a London mistress – like tommy-rot?

Hopefully, we have gone some way to explaining the interrelatedness of Shakespeare's profoundest philosophic thoughts and his maturest emotions that form the deeply poetic structure of his set of 154 sonnets as the basis for his poems and plays. By listening to the sonnets and respecting their evident structure we have been able to follow Shakespeare as he reveals his mature insights and feelings.

The step by step presentation in this essay invents nothing because it adheres rigorously to the evidence available in Q – as published in 1609. So a summary of the steps Shakespeare lays out in the sonnets seems in order as we conclude our journey into the heart of Shakespeare's mind.

We have seen that nature and the sexual dynamic of female and male are givens whose unconditional status is recognised when Shakespeare makes them the structural basis of his set of 154 sonnets and its two internal sequences[130]. Shakespeare bases his exploration and expression of mature love in all his plays and poems on this logical relationship. As we are part of nature then human love is incipient in nature and the sexual dynamic.

When we enter the sonnet set, the first fourteen sonnets encountered form the increase group. As the potential for increase follows on from the division of male from female in nature, Shakespeare argues that any form of human love must

---

[130] *The templates pictured in these footnotes may be useful for those who prefer to visualize the patterns of connectivity.*

The relationship between nature and the sexual dynamic can be represented by a template in which nature gives rise to the female with her male offshoot. For Shakespeare, nature is the basis for all forms of love:

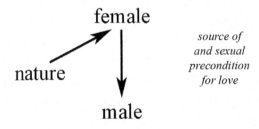

take as its generating condition the logic of increase otherwise love is selfish rather than interpersonal[131].

By addressing the possibility of writing in sonnets 15 to 19, Shakespeare recognises the implications of writing both for saying something about the physical process of increase and for his ability to communicate his understanding of truth and beauty and express his emotions. Unless the implications of writing are taken into account, a poet's philosophic verse cannot evoke mature love[132].

We move next to the Mistress sequence both because she is a logical unity and because of the decidedly separate treatment of beauty and then truth in her sequence. We find first that mature love is conditional on the Poet appreciating the logic of incoming sensations to the mind through the sensory organs. Then, second, the Poet shows through conversation with the Mistress that mature love depends on the ability of the female and male to use language fully cognizant of its capacity to represent or misrepresent through swearing or forswearing. So the Mistress sequence presents the connection between indiscriminate love based in sensory attraction and fully articulate love between willing lovers[133].

Armed with the logic of incoming sensations and the logic of language learned from his encounter with the Mistress, the Poet then proceeds to instruct the male youth (or the masculine side of the female). In the Master Mistress

---

[131] *The next step sees the male return to the female for the purpose of increase. Acknowledging the logic of increase is the crucial conscious act that makes possible the development of mature love:*

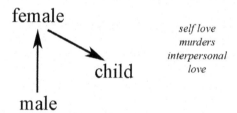

self love murders interpersonal love

[132] *The legendary reflexivity of Shakespeare's writing is engendered by his recognition that human increase is the logical precondition for writing and that writing is dependent on increase for its contents:*

poetry derives from the sexual dynamic of increase

[133] *Because sensory 'beauty' involves singular impressions and 'truth' involves the 'endless jar' between true and false, the import of the Mistress sonnets can be represented in a template for beauty/truth that corresponds in form to the nature/sexual template:*

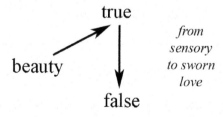

from sensory to sworn love

sequence he argues for the logic of truth by presenting the case for a nature-based understanding of love and critiquing the youth's propensity to fall for praise that has no substance when it short-circuits the natural dynamic of language. The Poet then separates language-based ideas in the mind (which he calls 'truth') from sensations and emotions generated in the mind by those ideas (which are wrongly called 'truth'). He argues that confusion over the logic of truth leads to the gravest errors in judgment and hence to the transformation of love to hate[134].

Then, in the later stages of the essay, we took account of the final two sonnets at the end of the Mistress sequence that complement the slave-making God mentality of the Master Mistress sequence with the 'little Love-God'. Shakespeare shows that erotic expression, which underpins all claims to extra-natural love (the biblical God), ironically identifies all such claims as derived from the sexual dynamic in nature[135].

As we emerge from Shakespeare's very determined presentation of the logic of the mind based in nature and the sexual dynamic, or what he calls truth and beauty, we become more conscious of the sexual/gender relationship between the female/male body dynamic and the feminine/masculine personae of the mind[136]. Because all Gods and Goddesses are but mind-based personae, and as Shakespeare locates them in the imagination, he points his finger at the literal belief in their existence as the primary cause of 'love hate'.

The female/male and feminine/masculine interchange is so significant that its confusion is at the heart of Shakespeare's histories and tragedies and its resolution is central to his comedies. Shakespearean love in its maturity is not only

---

[134] *The companion truth/beauty template to the beauty/truth template shows that the dynamic of true and false ideas can be sublimated in the mind as intuitions or emotions – and then expressed in poetry. The shift is from the dynamic of true and false to the singular affects experienced in the mind, which Shakespeare also calls beauty:*

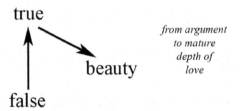

[135] *The relationship between the sexual (encompassing the female/male dynamic and increase) and the erotic (including the sensory, conceptual and imaginative) spans the evolutionary journey from the physicality of the body to the mentality of the mind. By accounting for both body and mind in the correct order in his set of philosophic sonnets, Shakespeare corrects the illogicalities of apologetic philosophers:*

the sexual is the precondition for the erotic - sonnets 153/154

[136] *The natural connection between the sexual dynamic of female and male and the gender dynamic of feminine and masculine should be at the center of any philosophy:*

the sexual body is the precondition for the genderised mind - sonnets 42/43,133/134, 143/144

a mature personal love but is the basis for the love between all his characters – and by extension all humankind[137].

The templates for nature, increase, beauty and truth, and truth and beauty can be combined to represent the logical arrangement of the 154 sonnets that together form the prerequisites for experiencing the mature form of love Shakespeare embeds in his set of sonnets[138] and dramatises in his plays.

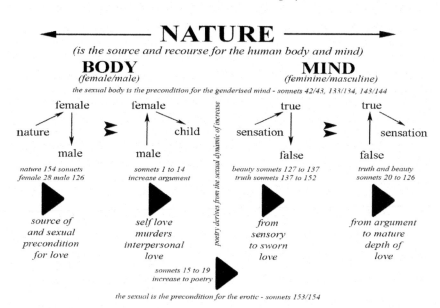

The evidence we have considered in this essay for an expression of Shakespearean love in his set of philosophic sonnets proves to be both deeply profound and fully comprehensive of human experience in nature – including the ideals generated in the mind. Little wonder then, if the 154 sonnets were published to present the philosophy behind all Shakespeare's poems and plays, his dramatic works particularly have exercised such a deep but barely understood hold both on everyday human activities and on the profoundest imaginings of the human mind[139].

---

[137] *The founding fathers of the United States appreciated the need to prevent any one religion based in imaginary Gods from taking power. They drafted the Declaration of Independence and the Constitution so that natural love could flourish unfettered by religious prejudice. Shakespeare anticipated such an eventuality but his rigorous sonnet philosophy and its mature expression of love also heralds an age where the precepts of the Constitution would be even more philosophically sound by accepting the natural relationship between females and males as inviolable.*

[138] *The above templates and insights can be combined into a nature-to-love template that lays out Shakespeare's conditions for mature love.*

[139] *Ironically, Hamlet has such a magnetic hold on the human imagination precisely*

Lytton Strachey predicted in 1905 that 'for its solution (the mystery of the *Sonnets*) seem to offer hopes of a prize of extraordinary value – nothing less than a true insight into the most secret recesses of the thoughts and feelings of perhaps the greatest man who ever lived'[140]. This brief essay shows that Shakespeare did reveal his profoundest thoughts in his set of 154 sonnets. On the evidence presented here (and in greater detail in *WSSP*), Shakespeare also manages to convey his deepest emotions. Because of the universality of his nature-based philosophy, they are the mature emotions basic to continued human well-being.

This essay points the way to an unprecedented prospect of entertaining a combination of Shakespeare's thoughts and feelings for the first time in 400 years. When the sonnet philosophy of 1609 is fully downloaded and embedded in thought and action, along with a sufficiently mature experience of love, Shakespeare's sonnets dissolve to reveal the living contents of his ideas and emotions.

Little wonder at this moment of increased global awareness many are turning to Shakespeare's works with the expectation that they offer, as Strachey intimates 100 years ago, a 'prize of extraordinary value' – the deepest of human 'thoughts and feelings' without compromise. Understanding Shakespeare's common sense philosophy is the key to accessing a mature experience of love brought to life by a poet, dramatist and philosopher with profound global insight.

---

because he reflects the common view of love and understanding that Shakespeare seeks to redress in his sonnets and in his powerful plays and poems. Shakespeare cast Hamlet purposefully as the archetypal soul on the border between the horrors of male-based beliefs and the maturity of his sonnet-based understanding and emotions. When Harold Bloom credits Shakespeare with 'the invention of the human' in creating thinking characters like Hamlet and Falstaff, he could not see into the distance beyond Hamlet represented in the sonnet philosophy. (Harold Bloom, *The Invention of the Human*, London, Fourth Estate, 1999.)

[140] *From:* Peter Jones, *Shakespeare Casebook,* London, Macmillan, 1977.